Reading Challenging Texts

Bringing together arts-integrated approaches, literacy learning, and classroom-based research, this book explores ways upper elementary, middle, and high school teachers can engage their students physically, cognitively, and emotionally in deep reading of challenging texts. With a focus on teaching about the Holocaust and Anne Frank's diary—part of the U.S. middle school literary canon—the authors present the concept of layering literacies as an essential means for conceptualizing how seeing the text, being the text, and feeling the text invite adolescents to learn about difficult and uncomfortable literature and subjects in relation to their contemporary lives. Offering a timely perspective on arts education advocacy, Chisholm and Whitmore demonstrate the vital need to teach through different modalities in order to strengthen students' connections to literature, their schools, and communities. Accessible strategies are illustrated and resources are recommended for teachers to draw on as they design arts-based instruction for their students' learning with challenging texts.

James S. Chisholm is Associate Professor of English Education in the College of Education and Human Development at the University of Louisville, USA.

Kathryn F. Whitmore holds the Ashland/Nystrand Chair of Early Childhood Research and is Director of the Early Childhood Research Center at the University of Louisville, USA.

Reading Challenging Texts

Layering Literacies Through the Arts

James S. Chisholm
and
Kathryn F. Whitmore

Co-Published by Routledge and
the National Council of Teachers of English

NEW YORK AND LONDON

First published 2018
by Routledge
711 Third Avenue, New York, NY 10017

and by Routledge
2 Park Square, Milton Park, Abingdon, Oxon, OX14 4RN

Routledge is an imprint of the Taylor & Francis Group, an informa business

© 2018 Taylor & Francis

The right of James S. Chisholm and Kathryn F. Whitmore to be identified as authors of this work has been asserted by them in accordance with sections 77 and 78 of the Copyright, Designs and Patents Act 1988.

Library of Congress Cataloging in Publication Data
A catalog record for this book has been requested

ISBN: 978-1-138-05863-7 (hbk)
ISBN: 978-1-138-05864-4 (pbk)
ISBN: 978-1-315-16406-9 (ebk)

NCTE stock number: 58644

Typeset in Minion Pro
by codeMantra

Dedicated to teachers who are brave, and becoming brave, about sanctioning challenging texts and topics in their classrooms

Contents

Contents

List of Figures

Foreword

The scene was set. Two hundred classmates and teachers sat waiting in the audience. In the front row was Fred Gross, a Holocaust survivor who had inspired the students with his family's survival stories just weeks before. Two eighth-grade students, who later described how apprehensive they were about performing, and whose teacher acknowledged their typical reluctance at school, walked to the front edge of the stage and each read a personal letter to Mr. Gross. Unexpectedly, Mr. Gross rushed to the stage with tears in his eyes to hug both girls. In this moment, these students discovered that although they knew Mr. Gross's words and story had affected them deeply, *their* words had the power to move him, too.

This was part of a culminating performance of a study that integrated the arts with Holocaust history and literature at one of four schools in a program called the Anne Frank: Bearing Witness Project, which involved a partnership with The Kentucky Center for the Performing Arts, Brown University's ArtsLiteracy Project, and the University of Louisville.

At another school four miles away, a different transformation took place. An eighth-grade student participated with her classmates in the arts-based Anne Frank study, but she had something more personal at stake. She was one of the only Jewish students in her class, and previously she downplayed her Jewish identity at school. During the project, she asked if she could bring her Rabbi to talk with the class and she began to wear a necklace with a Star of David to school every day.

These are just two of the many powerful learning experiences that took place in the Anne Frank: Bearing Witness Project, which James and Kathy expertly evaluated, researched, and wrote about in this important book.

As an arts education director for a leading performing arts center, I am frequently asked to demonstrate the value of teaching the arts and integrating the arts across subjects such as social studies and English. Education and funding communities increasingly request evidence in numerical form. How can you ascribe a number to quantify the impact on two 14-year-olds discovering that their voices as writers have the power to move others to tears? How can you measure the importance of a middle school student finding the courage and resolve to show who she really is in a school environment for the first time? I find that the most important and nuanced evidence of growth does not always lend itself to that kind of measurement.

Yet it was important for us to report to the Jewish Heritage Fund for Excellence, our funder, the ways in which their investment in this project had achieved its goals. James and Kathy went far beyond confirming *that* students were engaging and emotionally investing in their learning, responding with empathy to Anne Frank's diary, and making personal connections between this difficult history and their world today. Through their fastidious and innovative research, they discovered ways to explain *why* and *how* this robust learning was taking place. And herein lies the significance of this book: they provide a path for understanding how the arts play a role in multilayered literacy learning experiences that result in increased levels of engagement, empathy, emotional understandings, and even empowerment to action.

Their research is solidly grounded in multimodal and sociocultural theories, in which they demonstrate how students make meaning through multiple literacies of seeing, being, and feeling the text (visual, embodied, and emotional literacies, respectively). This is true for both processing new understandings and for communicating and expressing those understandings through various modalities.

At the heart of our work is a process developed at Brown University's ArtsLiteracy Project called The Performance Cycle, which is especially well-suited to tackling difficult and uncomfortable subject matter, and what James and Kathy call "challenging texts," because it provides powerful ways to develop a classroom culture in which students support each other as they share a deeper level of vulnerability and authenticity than they are usually asked for in school. Trust must be established. As The Performance Cycle continues, students become partners in constructing the curriculum, and they become more invested as learners.

The Performance Cycle not only uses the arts as a pathway into the curriculum—it also invites students to communicate their understandings artistically to classmates and others. In an especially compelling culminating performance, two students responded to the essential question "What is your humanity footprint?" by connecting the marginalization and oppression of Jews in Anne Frank's diary with shame, body image, and eating disorders. They choreographed and performed a dance using a tape measure as a prop to illustrate their message. The creative components of the Performance Cycle can yield cathartic and healing results when students allow themselves to share something inside that is painful. By taking the pain outside of themselves and manipulating it artistically, they discover that they have a power over it; by sharing their artistic work, they provide hope and courage to others. In this book, James and Kathy offer compelling arguments for teaching difficult and uncomfortable subjects and challenging texts, as well as numerous success stories from actual classrooms.

In this age in which instruction is heavily directed by what can be measured, *Reading Challenging Texts: Layering Literacies Through the Arts* offers a timely perspective with strong implications for arts education advocacy. James and Kathy explain how the arts catalyze robust learning experiences. They also demonstrate how students take their learning further when they engage in creative responses, which provides educators with windows through which more can be discovered about student learning. With many detailed examples, they explain the phenomena of layered understandings through different modalities that arts integration provides. This book is more than a study of successful classroom practices—it is an illuminating contribution to the field of educational research and practice.

Jeffrey Jamner, DMA
Senior Director of Education & Community Engagement
The Kentucky Center for the Performing Arts

Preface

When James was a 16-year-old American high school exchange student in Germany, his history class focused entirely on the First and Second World Wars. He recalls his visceral responses that this context created: *My heart would race when we discussed World War II. Since I was still learning the language, images, propaganda posters, maps, and graphs became crucial elements of my learning and reading in that class. And I learned a word that semester that comprised for me the learning goal for that course: Vergangenheitsbewältigung—coming to terms with the past. How do individuals and societies collectively come to terms with the atrocities of the Holocaust as they/we move toward less disturbing futures?*

Recently, when James visited the Anne Frank House in Amsterdam as a literacy researcher, he reflected in a diary entry: *Yellow/Orange-ish wallpaper adorns many of the rooms throughout the annex. Anne's room was very narrow, and I couldn't take my eyes off of the artifacts that had been affixed to her wall. Newspaper clippings included a spectacular image of Ginger Rogers. Also noteworthy for me was an image of Rembrandt's Portrait of an Old Man—[my family and I] had spent the afternoon that day at the Rijksmuseum where we sketched, among other paintings, Rembrandt's famous "Night Watch." The artifacts adorning Anne's bedroom walls were so diverse and reflected so many different interests. It was such a testament to the fact that people make their surroundings as familiar as they can even in the most unthinkable of circumstances. Anne's artifacts also served to represent her identities as a [Dutch] teenager, a writer, and an artist.*

Kathy recalls her first encounter with Anne Frank's diary as a young teenager: *In junior high school, Anne's diary was my introduction to the Holocaust. I have vivid memories of how the smooth, wooden seat felt under me in the darkened auditorium as I watched a black-and-white film based on the diary after we finished the book. Watching trucks marked with swastikas and hearing the eerie sound of sirens brought the haunting words in Anne's diary to life before my eyes and ears.* Kathy remembers how years later, while researching literature study groups in a third-grade classroom (Whitmore & Crowell, 1994), *the children held each other, arm-in-arm as they read Christopher Gallaz and Roberto Innocenti's* Rose Blanche *(1985), a sensory-rich Holocaust picturebook filled with terrifying and beautiful illustrations of Rose's experiences in Nazi Germany, and other picture and information books. The third-graders debated the ambiguities of the ending of* Rose Blanche *and vowed that they would have hidden their friend Aaron, the only Jewish child in the group, had they lived during those times.*

Inherent in our recollected initial encounters with Anne Frank and the Holocaust is the confluence of feeling and thinking surrounded by a multimodal ensemble that created lasting impressions on us, and enduring moral questions for us to consider throughout our lives. Visual maps in the history classroom, the tangible wall artifacts in the Anne Frank House in Amsterdam, and the sounds of the sirens in a film adaptation of Anne Frank's diary shaped our emotional responses and influenced our meaning-making experiences. As a reader, you might now be re-appreciating the sensory experiences of your own unique encounter with Anne Frank's diary or other challenging texts that caused you to think and feel in profound ways. We invite you now and throughout this book to consider how those moments are imbued with visual imagery, physical and visceral embodied perceptions and movements, and deep-seated—perhaps troubling—emotions. What implications might these realizations have for literacies learning in K-12 classrooms today? How do these realizations inform your role as a teacher when students have similar experiences?

ORGANIZATION OF THE BOOK

In this book, we offer an arts-based pedagogical approach to promote inquiry and enduring understandings for adolescents whose learning about Anne Frank is re-contextualized in 21st-century contexts. We organize the approach according to visual, embodied, and emotional literacies (although we recognize the overlap of these categories) that engage learners in seeing, being, and feeling the text. Each of Chapters 2–4 begins with a vignette, followed by classroom narratives of active and arts-based learning strategies that highlight how *seeing, being,* and *feeling the text* supports eighth-graders' engagement with Anne Frank's diary (which we often refer to as *The Diary*) and other challenging texts.

Chapter 2 focuses on three visual arts-related instructional strategies—Cordel, Icons, and Archives—that provide opportunities for learners to represent, read, create, recreate, and ultimately deepen meaning by *seeing the text*. The Cordel, a simple string stretched across one side of a classroom, is a place for learners to enter into challenging texts through photos and words. Icons are pieces of visual art, initially created by students in response to words, and later prompts for process drama. In Archives, students juxtapose images from their own family photo albums with Jewish families' photos in the first half of the 20th century, resulting in their relational and historical learning about individual lives before, during, and after the Holocaust.

In Chapter 3, we address the question, "What does it mean to *be the text*?" and share arts-based techniques that emphasize the body's role in literacies learning. Tableau and Pantomime invite students to position and move their bodies in ways that convey meanings of written texts to an audience (typically their classmates). In Sculpture Garden, students mold each other's bodies into shapes and stances to express meaning in response to excerpts of texts. Dramatic and Staged Performances are scenes that are composed, rehearsed, revised, and performed to share with others. These collaborative process drama strategies help us see how learners use their bodies to mediate thinking about challenging texts.

Chapter 4 draws on the role of emotion in literacies learning and focuses on how students reading challenging texts *feel the text*. In Creating Thick Air, firsthand interactions with Holocaust survivors contextualize the event historically and elevate the emotional intensity. Contemporary Connections are parts of dramatic performances in which students use music, dance, and spoken word to relate the content of challenging texts to their contemporary lives. And Marquee is a strategy to engage the broader school community in lessons from challenging texts. In our narrative, the Marquee becomes a call to action when an act of vandalism results in students' heightened desire to promote unity in their community.

In Chapter 5, our colleague, Eileen Landay, co-founder with Kurt Wootton of the Arts-Literacy Project at Brown University, contextualizes their instructional framework—The Performance Cycle—for use with challenging texts, including Anne Frank's diary. Eileen describes, specifically, and with compelling examples, ways to invite students into an arts-based community.

Our literacy colleague at The University of Iowa, Renita Schmidt, provides a critical synthesis of picturebooks and adolescent Holocaust literature in Chapter 6. Teachers may consult this synthesis to pair challenging texts with *The Diary of a Young Girl* to develop extended units of study related to the Holocaust. This critical review of literature is organized around the central concepts of *seeing, being,* and *feeling the text*—the foci of Chapters 2–4.

Chapter 7 applies our approach to *seeing, being,* and *feeling the text* through the arts to three popular challenging texts: *The Absolutely True Diary of a Part-Time Indian* (Alexie, 2007), *The Skin I'm In* (Flake, 1998), and *Enrique's Journey* (Nazario, 2013). We describe each selection using our criteria for challenging texts and highlight the particular ways in which *seeing, being,* and *feeling the text* can support robust reading experiences. We demonstrate how visual, embodied, and emotional strategies used with *The Diary* can be adapted for the purposes of studying these widely used challenging texts. We include additional teaching resources that promote layering literacies through the arts.

Chapter 8 highlights how and why arts-based literacy engagements position students to approach the Holocaust with respect. In their reflections on how they engaged with challenging texts and each other throughout their study of *The Diary*, adolescents show us how they "stand next to" Anne. Students demonstrate how they are interested in and capable of learning with challenging texts. We close by raising new questions about the Holocaust and theory and pedagogy about layering literacies with challenging texts.

Special Features

In this book, we link arts-based approaches to literacies learning with examples that allow readers to imagine themselves as teachers and students inside the classrooms we describe, particularly via photographs of compelling moments of engaged and embodied learning. Additionally, we offer brief teacher perspectives, culled from interviews and presentations by teachers in the project, and presented in "Teacher Voice" boxes in many chapters. These excerpts reveal teachers' worries, delights, questions, and insights. "Student Voice" boxes complement the teachers' perspectives by amplifying students' perceptions of their arts-based engagements with challenging texts.

We also include an example of multimodal assessment for arts-based instruction that we developed in the classrooms. We describe the Visual Learning Analysis (VLA) in Chapter 1 and use examples throughout the chapters. The VLA creates a pedagogical space within which students can teach their teachers and us about how they learn through visual, embodied, and emotional layers.

Lastly, three Appendices offer resources for educators. Appendix A includes directions for all of the arts-based strategies featured in the book. Appendix B, created by Renita, is a list of recommended picturebooks, information books, and adolescent literature about the Holocaust, organized by genre. Appendix C, which we co-created with Renita, is a list of contemporary texts we recognize as likely to be challenging in many school communities. You may consider adopting these for your own pedagogical purposes.

OUR PERSPECTIVES AS LITERACY RESEARCHERS

Anne Frank's diary was first published 70 years ago. And although *The Diary* has been taught in countless numbers of classrooms for generations now, having been translated into 70 different languages ("The diary at 70," 2017), there has been in the educational research literature relatively few accounts of teachers and students as they engage deeply with this topic. Despite the fact that the study of the Holocaust is mandated in curriculums in many states and countries across the world, there are few research-based portraits of the complexity of teaching this topic in classrooms in which teachers and students are striving to teach and learn this content deeply (e.g., see Gray, 2015; Juzwik, 2009; Schweber, 2004; Spector, 2007 for notable, empirical exceptions). As Schweber (2006) notes, "While hundreds of articles and an increasingly large number of books advocate Holocaust education, only very few of these base recommendations for practice on empirical research" (p. 51). Through this book, we seek to contribute to this literature by documenting and sharing the efforts of teachers, teaching artists, and students in our community who have found in the arts a means of mediating teaching and learning about challenging texts. Our focus on visual, embodied, and emotional literacies to teach challenging texts and our corresponding illustrations of classroom practice emerge from our analysis of students and teachers across varied classroom contexts striving to do justice to an important topic.

As qualitative educational researchers, we recognize how our own beliefs, histories, life experiences, and identities (influenced by race, gender, ethnicity, class, among other powerful social forces circulating in our society) shape how we view the world and how we interpret interactions in classrooms. To portray a more complete picture of how who we are shapes what we see and the meanings we interpret, we share here briefly our own positionalities, including the recognition that we are not Jewish. Nor are we Holocaust survivors, descendants of survivors, or Holocaust scholars. We are not arts educators. We are, however, literacy educators who desire to understand how to teach children and adolescents about issues of inequity in contemporary and historical contexts. We recognize that it won't be long until the survivors of the Holocaust are no longer with us to tell their stories firsthand. We take up the cause to help young people "bear witness" to the narrative of the Holocaust, and to other narratives that can help us develop critical consciousness about power and justice.

As we learn and write about Anne Frank and how teachers and students in our own community study the Holocaust, we consider our language choices carefully. Although we may not make the right decision in each example in this book, we choose not to appropriate language that was used by Nazis to frame the Holocaust (e.g., "Final Solution," "extermination"). Rather, we seek to use language that is authentic to each context where we conduct the research and respect the complexities of the realities of perpetrators, victims, resisters, and bystanders. For cogent discussions of the etymological complexities inherent in the language people use to talk about the Holocaust (including the problematic linking inherent in the term Holocaust itself), see Gray (2015) and Schweber and Findling (2007).

We recognize and appreciate that there are as many opinions about how to teach or not teach challenging texts as there are ways to teach. For example, simulations are generally recognized as a teaching method to avoid when approaching Holocaust history and literature, but Schweber (2004) portrays very positively a teacher who uses simulation effectively to evoke emotional learning for her students. In the end, as our colleague Fred Whittaker notes, teachers in each and every context are charged with the responsibility of bringing students safely into and out of their studies of the Holocaust. We offer this book as a resource for teachers who choose to take this journey with their students with care.

REFERENCES

Alexie, S. (2007). *The absolutely true diary of a part-time Indian*. Illus. E. Forney. New York, NY: Little, Brown and Company.

Flake, S. (1998). *The skin I'm in*. New York, NY: Hyperion Books.

Gallaz, C., & Innocenti, R. (1985). *Rose Blanche*. Illus. R. Innocenti. Mankato, MN: Creative Editions.

Gray, M. (2015). *Teaching the Holocaust: Practical approaches for ages 11–18*. New York, NY: Routledge.

Juzwik, M. M. (2009). *The rhetoric of teaching: Understanding the dynamics of Holocaust narratives in an English classroom*. Cresskill, NJ: Hampton Press.

Nazario, S. (2013). *Enrique's journey: The true story of a boy determined to reunite with his mother (Adapted for young people)*. New York, NY: Random House.

Schweber, S. (2004). *Making sense of the Holocaust: Lessons from classroom practice*. New York, NY: Teachers College Press.

Schweber, S. (2006). "Holocaust fatigue": Teaching it today. *Social Education, 70*(1), 48–55.

Schweber, S., & Findling, D. (2007). *Teaching the Holocaust*. Los Angeles, CA: Torah Aura Productions.

Spector, K. (2007). God on the gallows: Reading the Holocaust through narratives of redemption. *Research in the Teaching of English, 42*(1), 7–55.

The diary at 70: Anne Frank: Her life and legacy. (2017, May). *Life, 17*(9).

Whitmore, K. F., & Crowell, C. G. (1994). *Inventing a classroom: Life in a bilingual, whole language learning community*. York, ME: Stenhouse Publishers.

Acknowledgements

We first acknowledge, with solemnity, the survivors, their descendants, and the more than six million Jews and millions of other souls who lost their lives in the atrocities of the Holocaust. We pledge to "bear witness" to their shared and individual stories through the best means we have at our disposal—teaching young people, so that the world does not forget this history, its complexity, and its connection to our present day; and encouraging teachers to do the same.

Our invitation to participate in the Anne Frank: Bearing Witness Project, which initiated the learning we share in these pages, came from our friend and colleague, Jeffrey Jamner. Jeffrey, we thank you and The Kentucky Center for The Performing Arts for giving us the means to learn, innovate, and co-create with you. We now consider the Performance Cycle pivotal to our way of thinking about the arts and literacy thanks to our new friends and colleagues, the ArtsLiteracy team of educators—Eileen Landay, Kurt Wootton, and Len Newman. The project described in these pages continues to deepen and widen thanks to your talents and insights. We are grateful to Renita Schmidt, on whose expertise we relied to recommend an array of high quality Holocaust literature for children and adolescents.

We thank the teachers and students in whose classrooms we spent hours every week for months at a time: Kim (JJ) Joiner, Fred Whittaker, Tiffany LaVoie, and Kelly Holland. These teachers and students were welcoming and generous, and from their willingness to take risks, be reflective, and include us we learned so much. We appreciate the principals who supported these teachers' decisions to participate in the project, as well as the other teachers and teaching artists who participated and willingly allowed us to observe and record.

A special thank you to Fred Gross. Fred regularly visits so many of the classrooms we reference in this book, sharing the story of his childhood escape from Nazi Europe, and deeply affecting hundreds of students each year.

At the University of Louisville, a team of support helped with large and small tasks associated with the research and preparation of the book. Research assistants and doctoral students Ashley Shelton Arnold, Irina McGrath, Jonathan Baize, Aly Jacobs, Emily Zuccaro, Christie Angleton, and Leah Halliday were engaged in various phases of the project, from data collection to page proof reading and indexing. We are deeply appreciative of the Early Childhood Research Center community of scholars, and for the funding that supported all phases of this work. Vicki Johnson-Leuze, was our ever-present admin extraordinaire, and responded to each of our requests for chasing down permissions, formatting, and record keeping with a smile and a discriminating eye for detail.

Our thanks to Ranen Omer-Sherman, Jewish Heritage Fund for Excellence Endowed Chair of Judaic Studies at the University of Louisville. Ranen's review of the sections of the book that share historical and religious content was invaluable to us, as was his consistent encouragement and support. Any omissions or mistakes are our own.

We are thankful to have had the opportunity to conceptualize this book with Naomi Silverman during the final months of her career that over the years deeply influenced literacy research and education. Along with the reviewers' insights and questions, Naomi's response to our initial manuscript pushed our thinking forward and inspired the voice, message, and organization of the final version of this book. Karen Adler, our editor at Routledge, was a steadfast source of support throughout the production process.

The co-publication of this book with Routledge and the National Council of Teachers of English (NCTE) will bring it into view for so many English language arts teachers and teacher educators. To that end, we thank Kurt Austin, for his belief in the project and enthusiasm for its contents throughout the production process, and Emily Kirkpatrick for her intention to engage teachers in learning about this work.

This project, and *Reading Challenging Texts: Layering Literacies Through the Arts*, would not have been possible without generous financial support from the Jewish Heritage Fund for Excellence. Jeff Polson, David Kaplan, and Tiffany Fabing embraced this project from its inception and "stood next to" us as we studied the power of the arts in engaging our community in Louisville in learning about Anne Frank and the Holocaust.

To Vandy Chisholm and Tom Barten: Thank you for learning with us every step of the way.

Credits List

The authors and publishers wish to thank those who have generously given permission to reprint borrowed material:

Figure 1.1 "Morning" by Penny Sisto. Courtesy of the artist.

Excerpts and digital images (Figure 2.10, Figure 3.1) from: Chisholm, J. S., & Whitmore, K. F. (2016). Bodies in space/bodies in motion/bodies in character: Adolescents bear witness to Anne Frank. *International Journal of Education and the Arts, 17*(5), 1–31. Retrieved from www.ijea. org/v17n5/. © James S. Chisholm and Kathryn F. Whitmore.

Excerpts and digital image (Figure 3.9) from: Chisholm, J. S., Whitmore, K. F., Shelton, A., & McGrath, I. (2016). Moving interpretations: Using drama-based arts strategies to deepen learning about *The Diary of a Young Girl. English Journal, 105*(5), 35–41. Copyright 2016 by the National Council of Teachers of English. Reprinted with permission.

Excerpts from THE DIARY OF A YOUNG GIRL: THE DEFINITIVE EDITION by Anne Frank, edited by Otto H. Frank and Mirjam Pressler, translated by Susan Massotty, translation copyright © 1995 by Doubleday, a division of Random House LLC. Used by permission of Doubleday, an imprint of the Knopf Doubleday Publishing Group, a division of Penguin Random House LLC. All rights reserved. Any third party use of this material, outside of this publication, is prohibited. Interested parties must apply directly to Penguin Random House LLC for permission.

Figure 2.1 © United States Holocaust Memorial Museum.

Figure 2.6 U. S. Holocaust Memorial Museum, courtesy of Robert A. Schmuhl.

Figure 2.13 U. S. Holocaust Memorial Museum, courtesy of Johanna Starkopf Brainin.

Figure 2.14 U. S. Holocaust Memorial Museum, courtesy of Emanuel (Manny) Mandel.

Figure 2.15 U. S. Holocaust Memorial Museum, courtesy of Leah Hammerstein Silverstein.

Figure 2.16 U. S. Holocaust Memorial Museum, courtesy of The Shtetl Foundation.

Figure 5.1 Reprinted by permission of Eileen Landay and Kurt Wootton, *A Reason to Read: Linking Literacy and the Arts* (Cambridge, MA: Harvard Education Press, 2012), p. 10. © 2012 President and Fellows of Harvard College.

Chapter 1

Layering Literacies for Teaching about Anne Frank and Other Challenging Texts

Join us in a classroom learning story:

Michael Schubert, the son of Holocaust survivors, stands as a guest speaker in front of a group of eighth graders. Cello music plays quietly in the background. Behind him are digital slides of huge murals that depict scenes and symbols from the Holocaust. Kim Joiner, the classroom teacher, controls the slide show from her laptop at the side of the room. Michael asks Kim to zoom in on one corner of a mural where concentration camp prisoners are located. He asks the students, "What's the first thing you notice about them?"

Jeremy says, "They're all bald." Michael seizes the response to prompt students to reflect on how important their hair is to their identities. "Does your hair say I want to stand out?" he asks. "Does it say I want to fit in? Does it say I want to be left alone? Look at each other's hair for a minute." Students look around at the diverse range of hairstyles, colors, and lengths in the room. Michael continues, "It's part of us, isn't it?" He pauses. "It's the first thing the Nazis took away. Another thing they took away was your name." Michael tells the students that Nazis dehumanized Jews by referring to them not by their names, but by the numbers tattooed on their arms. He zooms in on that part of the mural, too.

"My mother," Michael continues, "when she was 18 years old, the first thing she did was have those numbers removed." Michael reflects on the scar that was left behind. "I still remember growing up, seeing this shiny spot on her arm where the numbers had once been. But my grandmother, she kept the numbers on her arm until the day she died."

Michael uses a book metaphor to explain to the students how differently his grandmother and his parents dealt with their memories of the Holocaust. His grandmother's story was an open book, which she would share with everybody—even Michael's roommate from college. Michael's parents' book from their life before and during the Holocaust, however, was closed. They would only occasionally (and sometimes unexpectedly) open it to tell a story. Michael then shares one story with Kim's students:

The Jewish high holidays celebrate the new year—Rosh Hashanah. We eat round challah. We dip it in honey, so you'll have a sweet year ahead. And it begins ten days of atoning for our sins that culminate in a holiday called Yom Kippur. Yom Kippur is the

Day of Atonement. And we fast on that day. There's this really, really important prayer called Kol Nidre, which you heard being played on cello as you came in to class today. Now, imagine this. Kol Nidre is considered one of the most beloved, holiest prayers of the year. The reason is historical. Many Jews over the centuries were forced by sword or by gun to convert. And so they lived their lives as a Catholic, as a Christian, as a Muslim, but they still felt Jewish inside. They were saying prayers that went against who they were. The all vows prayer, Kol Nidre, absolved them of any pledges, or promises, that they made that they did not or could not keep. It's a very, very special prayer. That's a little bit of a background on this.

So, I'm sitting in the synagogue with my mother. I was in my 20s. And the prayer service is very long and some of it is in Hebrew and some of it is mumbled. And you follow along and your thoughts wander. And my mother leans over to me and she asks, "Are you going to Kol Nidre with us next week? Let me tell you what Kol Nidre means to me." And that was the opening of that book that's usually closed.

"It was 1944 and they were killing all of the Hungarians in Auschwitz. It was just the most horrible time. The Nazis were speeding up the killings. The ovens were burning around the clock. Morale was as low as it had ever been. And at night, when the lights went out in the barracks and there was no talking—you could be severely punished if you did. It was the night before Yom Kippur. Again, this was the worst of times. The Nazis were diverting funds from their own defense to speed up the killings in the concentration camps. On this night, on the eve of Yom Kippur, in the silence a single man's voice was heard in the distance."

Michael begins to hum the melody of the Kol Nidre. The classroom is still and silent. *It was the Kol Nidre. "Soon other voices joined in."* Michael sings: *Kol Nidre/Ve'esarei/Vekonamei/Vekonamei.*

"And before you knew it other voices joined in." Michael's voice increases in volume as he sings: *Vekinuyei/Vekinusei … lo shevuot.*

"And before you knew it, all of the barracks were singing at the top of their lungs." Michael's voice increases volume again: *D'indarna.*

And my mother turned to me and said, "You know what, nobody heard us." Which was her way of saying, nobody punished us. Nobody stopped us. And at that moment I was sitting next to my mother and she said, "Nobody heard us." I took her hand and looked up—as if to God—and said, "Somebody heard you." It was a very special moment.

That was an example of defiance. It was an example of resistance. It was an example of how the community coped with this unbelievable trauma. It was a beautiful story. I'll never think of Kol Nidre any differently.

***

Michael's engagement with the students in Kim's classroom includes visual arts (the mural), musical arts (the recorded cello music), and dramatic arts (Michael's storytelling). It also illustrates the central concepts we explore in this book: visual, embodied, and emotional ways of teaching and learning about challenging texts. Michael's presentation engages his entire person—body and mind—to communicate his received story as a child of Holocaust survivors.

He and his story then become a new multimodal text that students see and feel in ways that we explore throughout this book.

In this book, we consider the power of the arts for teaching adolescents using challenging texts, particularly in relation to their contemporary lives. We show how layering the arts deepens student engagement by activating learners' entire bodies in confronting texts that demand our attention. "A layered experience is one in which the student's work moves across expressive mediums and becomes increasingly complex" (Landay & Wootton, 2012, p. 148). We illustrate layering literacies through visual (seeing), embodied (being), and emotional (feeling) texts in middle-school classrooms as teachers engage their students physically, cognitively, and emotionally in deep reading and empathetic response.

The core of this book is our description of a set of drama-, visual arts-, and movement-infused teaching and learning classroom engagements that support adolescents' understanding about the Holocaust through a variety of texts. These engagements occur in four classrooms in Louisville, Kentucky. The students we describe learn about historical events during the Holocaust as they read and respond to Anne Frank's diary, other Holocaust expository and poetic texts, survivors' first account stories, a variety of photographs and other visuals, and a play in script and staged forms. Alongside this content- and literature-driven learning about historical events, the students generate productive insights about social-emotional issues in their current lives as adolescents.

The Diary of a Young Girl (Frank, 1952), which we refer to as *The Diary*, is part of the literary canon in U.S. middle schools and is for many students their first and perhaps only encounter with the Holocaust (Magilow & Silverman, 2015; Prose, 2009). As the number of Holocaust survivors dwindles and living testimonies cease to exist, it is critical that young people develop the confidence and competence to carry on stories of hope and remembrance. Remembering involves understanding history and taking up contemporary moral lessons (Gray, 2015). Yet, innovative and powerful approaches to the study of Anne Frank and the Holocaust remain too infrequently realized in middle grades classrooms.

MEET THE TEACHERS

The four teachers with whom we learn about arts-based instruction with challenging texts work with students in four varied middle schools. (We refer to the educators in this book by their actual names.) Kim Joiner teaches drama at a large and diverse, public arts magnet school. A former English Language Arts teacher with a background in television and video production, Kim describes her teaching as "a little unconventional" and herself as "a high energy person." She stresses the importance of building community in her arts-based pedagogy, "We are artists and we make ourselves vulnerable all the time." She says this in order to guide students in critiquing their own and others' art. Kim challenges her students during their study of Anne Frank and the Holocaust to consider their lives after they leave her school: "If these walls could talk, what would they say about you? And not just when people are watching but when people are not watching."

Fred Whittaker teaches science and religion at a Catholic school. His school serves predominantly White and middle-class students in the center of an economically vibrant section of the city. Fred identifies how both science and religion appeal to him since they "allow students to be involved in interior journeys." He describes how a single student's question about the Holocaust "opened the flood gates" and how it instigated his initial, brief study of the Holocaust at the end of the year in his science classroom. That brief study is now a very popular semester-long course. Fred highlights how teaching about the Holocaust allows students to reflect on "who we can be as healers as opposed to people who create cruelty." He explicitly and often articulates his respect for students: "[They have] great emotional intelligence … they have an ability to inhabit some complex lessons from our studies of morality and the theology that's inherent in Holocaust education." Although engaging in drama-based inquiry activities is new to Fred, he embraces continuous learning as a teacher and compares some of his most powerful learning experiences with shaking a snow globe and having his world turned upside down. And with regard to innovating teacher practice, Fred recognizes that "sometimes we teach best when we're off balance."

With undergraduate and graduate degrees in acting, Tiffany LaVoie teaches drama at a mid-size and diverse, public arts magnet school. She characterizes her teaching as "the most important job in the world" and clarifies that she's "not raising 28 actors—that's not how I approach the classroom. I'm learning and growing with 28 young adults that are about to become parts of our society, just helping [them] … be successful." Despite being relatively unfamiliar with *The Diary* and approaches to teaching about the Holocaust, she found in the arts-based approach discussed in this book "the essence of the human story behind it." Tiffany enjoys working with students in eighth-grade, in particular, because "they're still open to play. And they still have a desire to play. And I like working with that age because, that is really where they're developing their personalities. They're trying on personae. And, so you have the opportunity to have an incredibly large impact; they haven't hardened their shells yet, they're still deciding what person they want to be."

A former education writer, Kelly Holland teaches English Language Arts at a large, "traditional" magnet middle school. Kelly's instructional strategies include Reader's Theater and Socratic Seminars, and her pedagogical philosophy emphasizes critical thinking and civic responsibility: "I feel passionately that [students] need to be taught how to think for themselves and form ideas and opinions and back them up, and become citizens regardless of what career path they choose." Kelly is committed to teaching at the middle-school level and positions her students as capable and compassionate. Although she does not typically read *The Diary* with her students, Kelly teaches about the Holocaust each year. Specifically, she draws on Teaching Tolerance (tolerance.org), which she incorporates in her curriculum.

Traditional schools in Louisville emphasize skills and academic achievement in highly structured settings. For example, the desks in Kelly's classroom are arranged in rows facing the teacher, affixed to the floor. We include this information not to criticize traditional classrooms *per se*, but to contrast them with Kim's classroom, in which desks don't even exist; Fred's classroom, in which considerable, choreographed effort is made to move large science lab tables to make space for process drama activities; and Tiffany's classroom, in which both moveable desks and a small theater stage are available.

We learn from each of these teachers different and powerful examples of learning through the arts. As you can appreciate, these teachers have both similarities and differences in their histories, disciplines, and pedagogical approaches. Our hope is that the composite profile for teaching and learning about Anne Frank and the Holocaust will provide a malleable structure that both new and seasoned teachers can use and adapt to engage their students in generative learning about difficult content using innovative arts-based practices.

To that end, we hope that you can see yourself and your students in the classrooms of Kim, Fred, Tiffany, Kelly, and the other teachers featured in this book. But we also hope that you can learn from the experiences we describe in classrooms that don't look like yours. As the teachers featured in this book note throughout their experiences using the arts to teach about the Holocaust, they learn invaluable lessons from the risks they take—working with new texts, exploring content outside of their disciplines, and experimenting with new, arts-infused pedagogical strategies.

In this book, we explore pedagogical and theoretical approaches to ambitious instruction about texts that are, for various reasons, challenging for teachers and students. Our pedagogical, or teaching, goals are to increase learners' engagement and to support teachers in moving toward offering students challenging texts. Our theoretical goals in this book are to explain why—including deepening understanding about layering literacies with arts-based instructional methods and generating insights into learning by privileging visual texts, the body, and emotion as mediating, omnipresent factors in classrooms. Our recommendations for guiding student learning about challenging texts, including Anne Frank's diary (and the wider Holocaust narrative), add to the pedagogical literature for educators and illuminate theoretical understandings about the role of the arts in critical literacy learning and teaching.

LAYERING LITERACIES: OUR LEARNING THEORY

We conceptualize our multimodal approach to teaching and learning about challenging texts as layering literacies. It involves two components that we adapt from Landay and Wootton (2012) and develop here. First, layering involves "movement across expressive mediums" (p. 148). Along with other thinkers (e.g. Jerome Harste, Gunther Kress, Theo van Leeuwen, and Marjorie Siegel) who foreground the value of the multiple modes through which students make meaning, we conceptualize this movement across mediums of expression as literacies learning. Yet, layering also involves the increasing complexification of students' work—whatever that work might be. Therefore, we examine the increasing complexity of student work through the lens of critical transactional theory about difficult knowledge, and accomplish this by drawing on theoretical insights from Louise Rosenblatt, Dennis Sumara, Deborah Britzman, and Cynthia Lewis.

Multimodal Social Semiotic Theory

In the field of English Language Arts education, there is clearly no longer one literacy. We understand that literacies are multiple; constructed with and inseparable from identities, cultures, bodies, histories, actions, and emotions; social; and political. In this book, we focus on the following (of the many possible) literacies as realized by varied verbal and nonverbal forms and texts:

- Visual literacies: Seeing the text
- Embodied literacies: Being the text
- Emotional literacies: Feeling the text

We situate our thinking about these literacies within multimodal social semiotic and critical transactional theories of learning. Multimodal social semiotic theorists like Kress and van Leeuwen (2001) consider the vast repertoires of meaning-making modes that teachers and students use every day in their classrooms as central to teaching and learning. Students constantly make and transform meaning through linguistic as well as gestural, musical, sculptural, and visual modes. As students make interpretations or compose texts across these multiple modes, they engage in the process of transmediation (Siegel, 1995; Suhor, 1984). For example, students might take in new knowledge by observing paintings (a visual text), and share their understandings in the form of a written blog (the linguistic mode). One power of transmediation is that it creates opportunities for students to generate new insights not necessarily available in a singular mode of meaning. Multimodal social semiotic theory is "concerned with how human beings make meaning in the world through using and making different signs, always in interaction with someone" (Stein, 2008, p. 875). Thus, multimodal social semiotic theory provides a useful lens through which to study arts-based learning with challenging texts because it privileges expressive mediums that have for millennia provoked powerfully productive responses to society and the human condition, and texts that can question the foundations on which people build their lives.

Visual Literacies

Although it has a long history in English Language Arts education, the visual mode has received increased attention of late, given more recognition of the importance of infographics and other graphical representations across content areas. Harste (2014) guides our rationale for the importance of the visual in teaching critical literacies, laying out four components in his argument for arts-infused literacies instruction:

> First, art encourages learners to see more differently, more aesthetically, more emotionally, more parsimoniously... Second, art affords critical expression... Third, art affords abduction—the exploration of possibility, creativity, and imagination... Fourth, art affords agency—the ability to impose a different order on experience.
>
> (pp. 96–97)

Our work emphasizes visual texts for reading and composing challenging texts—particularly as they relate to the Holocaust. Integrating visual texts from the Holocaust into classroom instruction presents especially complex and ethical dilemmas for teachers. And although visual arts-based curricula may not be entirely "new" to some readers in the literacy research and teaching community, the instructional strategies and reflections on learning we present in Chapter 2 will be new to many practicing and preservice classroom teachers and teacher educators.

Embodied Literacies

We want teachers to invite students to get up, out of their seats, and move their bodies in place and around the classroom. And we want teachers to join them (Cahnmann-Taylor & Souto-Manning, 2010). Although much research explores and theorizes the embodied nature of all learning (Claxton, 2015), we focus in this book on bodies in movement. Educators demonstrate how bodies are instrumental in engaging people in their learning processes (Edmiston, 2014; Landay & Wootton, 2012) since emotion happens in the body and "we learn more effectively when we learn in an emotional, embodied manner" (Woodcock & Hakeem, 2015, p. 17). As we illustrate in Chapter 3, embodied arts-based literacies learning mobilizes the body as a primary vehicle for meaning making (Eisner, 2002) for participants, who, in turn establish themselves as signs (or texts) to be interpreted by audience members who hear, see, feel, and read the bodies of their classmates to construct their own meanings.

Emotional Literacies

Emotional literacies allow placing one's body and mind in the context of another, thereby affording learners multiple perspectives on texts and the capacity to draw on those perspectives to act in the world. Along with Lewis and Crampton (2016), we "view emotion as an *action* that involves social actors and mediating signs or tools such as language, texts, bodies (gestures), objects, and space" (p. 105, emphasis in original). Adolescents in the middle-school classrooms featured in Chapter 4 express appreciation for the ways transacting with visual and embodied texts support their empathy for Anne Frank and her family, and the many other individuals who experienced the Holocaust in varied ways. They further share with us that their increased empathy mediates their emotions about contemporary issues in their own lives and the lives of others. For example, students write and perform texts that criticize rape culture in the United States, debate perceptions about what it means to be a Black girl, and explore the social roots of anxiety- and eating-related disorders. Using Anne Frank as a starting point, students and teachers talk about the "missing" and "invisible" people in the world today. They name them and they consider how they can make such people visible to society. These connections develop after months of working with Anne Frank's diary and arts-based learning strategies. We believe that the approach we describe in this book allows students and teachers to work toward enduring understandings about whatever challenging texts and issues they choose to take up.

Critical Transactional Theory

Layering literacies is also informed by the seminal transactional theory which explains the reading process as centered in meaning-making, the written word as reflective and transformative of the world, and readers as meaning-makers as they take aesthetic and efferent (Rosenblatt, 1978) and critical (Lewis, 2000) stances toward a text. Readers focus their attention differently during aesthetic and efferent readings and can take these different stances toward the same text. Briefly, Rosenblatt (1978) argues that readers focus their attention on "living through" (p. 25) experiences during aesthetic readings and on what they will "carry away" (p. 24) from efferent readings. These stances occur on a continuum; readers who acquire information during efferent readings may also engage vicariously with characters' experiences during aesthetic readings. The transactional theory is especially relevant for studying how learners transact with Anne Frank's diary since readers of her writing often reflect on its beauty and elegance while also considering the difficult and disturbing historical moment in which she wrote. Her diary, in other words, occasions an ideal space for readers to take both aesthetic and efferent stances as they transact with the text.

Critical transactional theory broadens Rosenblatt's ideas to include the political and social dimensions of texts and responses to them, in order to push readers to consider dominant and embedded discourses of privilege, oppression, and racism (Lewis, 2000). We highlight a critical literacy perspective (Janks, 2009) in our analysis of the complexity of students' transactions with texts that ask always and everywhere: Whose voice is privileged/whose story gets to be told? Whose voice is silent? Whose stories are absent? Adding the critical layer to literacies learning broadens readers' transactions with texts beyond personal connections and resists simplifications about victims, perpetrators, resisters, and bystanders (Gray, 2015). Britzman (1998) argues that students who read Anne Frank's diary encounter pain in her words and respond to that pain by developing questions about what it means to be a victim, perpetrator, resister, and bystander.

WHAT ARE "CHALLENGING TEXTS"?

The theoretical foundation for our work helps us think about the conceptual and practical complexities of teaching and learning with challenging texts in adolescent classrooms. A critical literacy perspective provokes increasingly complex and embodied thinking that leverages emotion as a mediating factor in learning "difficult knowledge" (Britzman, 1998). As Sumara (2002) points out in his argument for the value of reading literature in schools: "we must continue to create interesting interpretive sites that both clarify and complicate what we believe to be true" (p. 8). Readers of Anne Frank's diary can learn *about* her life and its historical context, and readers can learn *from* her by developing insight into Anne's life and history and their own lives.

Insights gained about and from Anne Frank's diary are beneficial. Yet, working with this and other challenging texts provokes discomfort and uncertainty for teachers and for students. Texts may be challenging and uncomfortable because (among many possibilities):

- the topic is taboo, or not sanctioned in schools (sexual orientation, death, divorce, violence, religion, etc. related to characters or plot lines);
- the teacher feels un- or underprepared for the content; or
- the content is emotionally troubling and contains "difficult knowledge" (Britzman, 1999; Zembylas, 2014).

The Holocaust, including Anne Frank's diary, fits all three criteria.

Taboo Topics in School

For some adults, the Holocaust and Judaism in general, and death camps and other atrocities more specifically, are forbidden topics for children and adolescents. At least four topics—death, genocide, religion, and sexuality—are implicit and often quite explicit elements of *The Diary of a Young Girl* which teachers must inevitably make instructional decisions as they engage with students as they read. Additionally, the literary genre of diary writing might not be acceptable for some teachers in certain contexts. They may feel the diary format of the text excludes male readers and privileges female readers (an idea with which we firmly disagree), or they may be worried about the possibility of students bringing stories about difficult topics into the classroom from their families or neighborhoods. Determining the boundary lines for what students can and cannot write in a diary, and interrogating gender ideologies, are factors that many teachers confront. Yet we argue, as does Jones (2006), that we cannot protect ourselves from fear, guilt, or sadness that we experience about taboo topics and difficult knowledge by silencing students or censoring topics out of classrooms. Rather, making space in school to sanction taboo topics, and the emotions that live alongside them, is a choice teachers must make.

Teacher Content Knowledge

You, like many teachers, may feel ill prepared to teach the historical content of the Holocaust and the implied religious content of Judaism, and do not feel knowledgeable enough to competently answer questions from students, parents, or administrators. (Some tough questions raised by students in Kim, Fred, Tiffany, and Kelly's classes are found in the Student Voice Box in this chapter.) Teachers who may not have educational backgrounds in cultural studies, religious studies, history, or social studies may feel a sense of nervousness when it comes to contextualizing *The Diary* within the historical events of the Holocaust.

A plethora of high-quality instructional materials exist on which teachers may draw to teach about the Holocaust. We reference such materials throughout this volume. To facilitate learning for teachers for whom this content is less familiar, the following resources are highly acclaimed:

- The University of Southern California Shoah Foundation's Institute for Visual History and Education (https://sfi.usc.edu/);
- The United States Holocaust Memorial Museum's website, *First Person* podcast series, and *Echoes of Memory* writing workshops for survivors of the Holocaust (www.ushmm.org/);
- Facing History and Ourselves (www.facinghistory.org/); and
- Yad Vashem: The World Holocaust Remembrance Center (www.yadvashem.org/)

All of these institutions support teachers who want to deepen their study of the Holocaust. Collaborations among social studies, humanities, arts, religious studies, and literature teachers around a study of the Holocaust can also be rewarding for both teachers and students who see the learning potential of cross-curricular content.

Student Voice Box

How could this genocide be allowed and how could it happen without any other nations knowing?

Danielle, eighth-grade student

How could we as people memorialize something so horrific but not notice it's still going on today?

Hannah, eighth-grade student

How were Jews treated after the Holocaust?

Allison, eighth-grade student

My question is who are the Anne Franks in this world today?

Sam, eighth-grade student

What would have happened if Anne Frank survived the Holocaust?

Hank, eighth-grade student

Emotionally Troubling Content

For all—including us as co-readers, researchers, observers, photographers, and writers—the Holocaust presents deeply troubling events, individual and collective stories, and overall sadness and anger. In fact, teaching the Holocaust can be painful for teachers and may explain why teachers sometimes move too quickly past the disturbing historical content to the personal narratives that might be read as more constructive than devastating (Prose, 2009).

Some adults ascribe to and express a discourse of innocence, which references the desire that children and adolescents be kept from knowing about emotionally troubling content. These well-meaning adults intend to protect young learners and assume that they aren't able to understand or engage with challenging topics. The discourse of innocence can be used as a primary mechanism of regulation by school administrators, teachers, and families, and serves as a rationale for censoring instructional materials that disrupt the status quo. We empathize with the desire to protect children and adolescents (and ourselves) from disturbing emotions and knowledge. And yet, we also commit, and encourage you to commit, to taking risks with emotionally challenging topics, so that classrooms can become places where young people can face troubling content with caring teachers.

WHY ENGAGING ADOLESCENTS WITH CHALLENGING TEXTS IS WORTH THE EFFORT AND THE RISK

We believe that *not* addressing the realities of the Holocaust may be more harmful than we realize because by treating students as in need of protection and stripping them of their agency, we fail "to give them the tools to prepare for democratic participation in a pluralistic world and we limit their perspective of what it takes to build an equitable society" (Ritchie, 2017, p. 61). Totten and Feinberg (2001) agree, arguing that to shield students from the discomfort of the whole story by studying only aspects of the Holocaust, such as the rescuers' roles or the lighter side of "hiding out," is miseducative.

Sometimes a particular text is highly challenging in one context, perhaps because of a more conservative community, and less challenging in another context, perhaps because of an individual teacher's interests and preparation. The teachers in our story share a desire to provide learners with invitations to think about challenging, sometimes previously taboo topics and texts. They range in levels of comfort and preparedness for teaching challenging texts about the Holocaust. One of the teachers, Fred Whittaker, has taught the Holocaust for many years and is a local expert about Holocaust education, but Fred had not previously introduced students to *The Diary*. Although more comfortable with the content, Fred was also new to arts-based instructional strategies. In contrast, as a drama teacher, Kim Joiner was quite comfortable with process drama strategies, yet expansion into visual arts and using *The Diary* as a text were new and required taking some risks. Other teachers were comfortable with challenging texts as a pedagogical concept, but the Holocaust content was new and a bit intimidating.

Teacher Voice Box

I think it intimidated me as I'm not a literature teacher and I think I really feared entering into a work that I hold as sacred and not being up to the task of disseminating that importance.

Fred Whittaker, science and religion teacher

When faced with a challenging text, some teachers might understandably want to omit details that are especially uncomfortable, and thus "certain [Holocaust] issues tend to be avoided, marginalized, repressed, or denied" (LaCapra, 1994, p. 23). As a result, the larger story of the Holocaust is revised. Britzman (1999) cautions that

> if the pedagogy of the Diary enacts the educator's desire for a rescue fantasy, stable truth, and the splitting of good and evil … we lose the chance to work through the ambivalences that are also a part of the crisis of witnessing
>
> (p. 304)

Before we move on from our discussion of challenging texts, we want to recognize that to decide to read such literature with students is an act of professional courage. Every student has the right to read and the "freedom to explore ideas and pursue truth wherever and however they wish" (National Council of Teachers of English, 2012). Further, young people have the right to see themselves and others in the literature they read—and to be able to step in and out of those vicarious experiences. And of particular concern for us, students deserve opportunities to question, enjoy, challenge, and learn about and from the literature they read for their entire lives. Reading challenging texts can promote students' learning about the world around them—locally and globally—and can motivate their interest in continuing to learn with literature (Groenke, Maples, & Henderson, 2010). When students learn about and from challenging texts, they learn to read the word and the world (Freire, 1970).

TEACHING ABOUT ANNE FRANK AND THE HOLOCAUST

We appreciate how clearly Prose (2009) sets out the challenge of teaching about Anne Frank and the Holocaust:

> And so it happens that teachers—undercompensated and overburdened by crowded classrooms—must assume yet another challenging task, one that seems essential for their students' historical, literary, and moral education. They must stand in front of a room of bright-faced young people and inform them that not very long ago, the German government and its army cold-bloodedly gassed and brutally murdered millions of Jews, gypsies, homosexuals, Poles, Jehovah's Witnesses, and political opponents, unless—in a very few cases—they managed to hide in caves and haylofts and attics, like the little girl whose book survived, though its young author did not.
>
> (p. 254)

Few challenging texts have received more attention for the ways in which their teaching has been approached than *The Diary*. Various editions of Anne Frank's diary and the numerous texts that have been based on it provide perspectives on how Anne's words and life ought to be understood and what Anne's legacy is or should be. Unfortunately, there are numerous examples of problematic ways *The Diary* has been taught in middle-school classrooms. In general, scholars of Holocaust studies describe problematic instructional approaches that sensationalize, sentimentalize, or romanticize Anne's story (Gray, 2015; Juzwik, 2013; Rubin, 2000; Schweber, 2004; Shawn, 1995; Spector & Jones, 2007; Totten & Feinberg, 2001). Some approaches shock students with graphic images or difficult-to-contextualize statistics about the devastation caused by the Nazi genocide of European Jews and others. Others trivialize or romanticize Anne's life as portrayed in the diary she kept. As perhaps an extreme but illustrative example, one student in the eighth-grade classroom studied by Spector and Jones (2007) concludes that Anne would likely be happy to be at a concentration camp because she could be outside in nature, "frolicking" (p. 36).

Clearly, despite the well-intentioned efforts of teachers to situate Anne's diary during this disturbing historical period, students may leave such lessons with broad misconceptions. Because *The Diary* may be the only extended exposure many people have to the Holocaust, the consequences for misrepresenting Anne's words and life are too severe to overlook. Instruction about *The Diary*, like most challenging texts and topics, demands intentional and informed curricular decision making.

There is consensus among teachers and scholars of Holocaust studies that simulations of any kind have no place in the classroom (USHMM, n.d.). Imagining that one has only minutes to pack all of one's belongings in one tiny suitcase, or standing in a tight space to simulate the experience of traveling in a cattle car, or skipping the lunch line to experience the hunger felt in concentration camps not only falls short of reproducing those experiences—for whatever purposes they might serve—but misleads students to believe that they actually understand what it was like to live through the Holocaust:

> Even when great care is taken to prepare a class for such an activity, simulating experiences from the Holocaust remains pedagogically unsound. The activity may engage students, but they often forget the purpose of the lesson and, even worse, they are left with the impression that they now know what it was like to suffer or even to participate during the Holocaust.
>
> (USHMM, n.d.)

We can't make the mistake of allowing students to think that now they (or we) know the agonies of the Holocaust; such pedagogical inclinations create trivial and inappropriate comparisons of pain (Gray, 2015). To examine the suffering of the people between 1933 and 1945 in no way leads to students having an accurate context to measure suffering today. Learning about the Holocaust is not meant to provide students with a way to compare their own pain and suffering; rather it is a catalyst that allows students to become informed, incite change, and to continue the stories of those who suffered.

Teacher Voice Box

The Holocaust's uncomfortable truth is that beasts, mad men, or monsters didn't create it; it was mainly perpetrated by, endured by, and witnessed by humans who were pretty much identical to us. What makes them identical is that they had free choice and they were going through the dynamics of choosing that we go through. And how do you take the students into that and allow them to comprehend that every day, decision by decision—yes by yes, no by no—these individuals became capable of this prejudice and genocide. It's an important dialogue to have that everyone in the Holocaust was a human being, just like us.

Fred Whittaker, science and religion teacher

With these goals to inform young people about the Holocaust, to promote societal change, to reject all forms of oppression, and to continue the stories of those who suffered and lived during this historical period, we aim to accomplish the following in this book:

- Share our learning from eighth graders about the instructional possibilities that exist in the experiences of arts-based readings of *The Diary* and other challenging texts;
- Provide support and encouragement for teachers who want to do justice to the content and history of *The Diary* and other challenging texts; and
- Deepen understanding about the layered nature of literacies learning, with a focus on visual, embodied, and emotional readings of multimodal texts.

We begin, though, by providing a brief background on *The Diary* and the broader Holocaust narrative as it is taken up in schools in the United States.

The Diary of a Young Girl: A Brief History

Although the earliest version of *The Diary* was written solely for herself—a chronicle of her coming of age, her time spent in the annex, and her negotiations with the lives surrounding her— Anne eventually explored through her diary her own writerly aspirations, evidenced by heavy revisions and self-edits in places throughout her journals. And Anne's writing was not contained to this one diary. Anne was a prolific and gifted writer, a fact that is too often overlooked in studies of *The Diary* in U.S. schools (Prose, 2009). In addition to her diary, Anne kept a book with lines from writers like Shakespeare and Goethe, quotations that she found interesting, and even words that resonated with her. She wrote fairy tales, short stories, and collected storylines for a novel (*Cady's Life*), which are collected in *Anne Frank's Tales from the Secret Annexe* (van der Stroom & Massotty, 2010).

Anne began to edit her own diary when she heard a Dutch government radio announcement from Minister Gerrit Bolkestein. Bolkestein, while in exile in England, encouraged listeners to keep accounts of their experiences during the war (Anne Frank House, 2013; Shandler, 2012). Anne's view of her diary as private quickly changed, and she created a second version that was "cleaned up" for public viewers (Magilow & Silverman, 2015). Anne's father, Otto Frank, was the only surviving member of Anne's family and of the eight total who hid in the annex with Anne. After the war, Otto Frank was given Anne's diary upon returning to the annex. He sought to fulfill his daughter's wish to be a published author and made additional edits, removing information about his family that he felt was of a sensitive nature, before seeking publication opportunities (Totten & Feinberg, 2001). Ultimately, Anne Frank's voice succumbed to a number of alterations before it reached the public (Shandler, 2012), which brings to light the important point that "all representations of the Holocaust are mediated, no matter how 'truthful' they may attempt—or claim—to be, and downplaying or denying this mediation risks distorting important information" (Magilow & Silverman, 2015, p. 29).

The Diary, as a mediated text, therefore, provides a starting point for readers of Holocaust accounts (Zapruder, 2002) and is now as readily identifiable as Anne's widely recognized school photo. As Zapruder notes, "For though Anne Frank had perished in the Holocaust, the survival of her diary could guarantee the symbolic survival of the writer herself" (p. 3). Readers initially saw Anne Frank's diary as a reminder that the human spirit can triumph over evil (Magilow & Silverman, 2015), a sentiment encoded in one of Anne's last entries, which includes *The Diary*'s most famous lines, from July 15, 1944: "It's a wonder I haven't abandoned all my ideals, they seem so absurd and impractical. Yet I cling to them because I still believe, in spite of everything, that people are truly good at heart" (Frank, 1952, p. 328). Fabric artist, Penny Sisto, pairs this famous line with her interpretation of Anne Frank's words. The quilt in Figure 1.1 is displayed at many of the Anne Frank: Bearing Witness Project events.

However, positioning *The Diary* only as an exemplar of the indomitable human spirit is potentially problematic. We counter this narrow reading with discussions and descriptions of additional Holocaust texts in Chapter 6 and throughout this book.

FIGURE 1.1 A likeness of Anne Frank, called "Morning," as conveyed in fabric art by Penny Sisto
Photo: Jeffrey Jamner.

One Life to Help Us Approach the Holocaust

Schweber (2004) says, "In order to represent this history fairly, some notion of the large numbers of victims, Jewish and otherwise, needs to be conveyed" (p. 101). At the epicenter of the Holocaust are six million Jews who were persecuted and murdered by the Nazis and their collaborators between the years 1933 and 1945—a staggering and abstract fact for all learners to grapple with and take in. In order to give the Holocaust meaning, relevance, and immediacy, teachers can distill and reduce the six million, the overwhelming facts and figures, the statistics, the math, the names, and the maps, to *one*. One life brings the history to life, because "a sense of the individuality of each victim needs to be conveyed" (Schweber, 2004, p. 101). When students understand that there was one person—like Anne Frank—among those many victims, they can find an access point to the Holocaust beyond mere information (Gray, 2015).

Fred Whittaker, an eighth-grade religion teacher, is a primary source for us for understanding Holocaust education. He introduces Anne Frank to his eighth-grade students like this:

I don't know how much you know about Anne Frank. Sometimes when we summarize things, it's horribly accurate, and sometimes its simplicity is horribly inaccurate. To say that she was a Holocaust victim is highly accurate. And to say that she lived part of her life in hiding is an incredibly powerful statement. I think we would all agree that that's the starting place for us. She was a teenager. She went into hiding. Someone betrayed her. And she was sent into the abyss of the Holocaust. I'm going to show you a collage of pictures of Anne Frank. It's the Anne Frank that everyone thinks about when we think about Anne Frank's diary. Anne Frank's diary is this beautiful voice of someone who's very much alive. Profoundly alive. Poetically alive. And she's left behind the observations she's made when she was in life. And they teach us a lot. As I show you this montage, I'd like you to write down things you might know about Anne Frank or questions you might have about Anne Frank.

The classroom study about the Holocaust that we describe in this book is an opportunity for students to engage with the diverse experiences of others, see themselves and their lives in the world, and consider how to act in the world in response to reading *The Diary* and other Holocaust texts. Beginning the study with one life guards against miseducation that results when students are presented with information that is too confusing or too sociohistorically distant to comprehend. It also guards against insulating students from the emotions and connections that allow them to learn more deeply about themselves and others.

Indeed, Prose (2009) notes that developing an emotional connection to Anne Frank promotes a contextualized reading of Nazi atrocities and the crimes against humanity that are perpetrated in genocides:

> The semblance of ordinary domesticity that the Franks preserved enables Anne's audience to read her story without feeling the desire to turn away, the impulse we may experience when we see the photos and footage of the skeletal dead and dying.
>
> (p. 171)

In many ways, the challenge of teaching about Anne Frank is a challenge of empathy. Teachers and students are asked initially to hold at arm's length the millions of victims, survivors, resisters, bystanders, and perpetrators as they create a relationship with one adolescent girl.

Student Voice Box

This is only one person's life we are reading about right now and we are already like experiencing all the emotions that she is going through. And just multiply that times six million and realize how many people had to go through this terrible part of history.

Arianna, eighth-grade student

The next three chapters illustrate classroom teachers and students exploring how the arts mediate visual, embodied, and emotional readings of one teenage girl's diary and other challenging Holocaust texts. In Chapter 2, we join Fred Whittaker's students as they debrief their trip to the United States Holocaust Memorial Museum and explore how they and other eighth-grade students in the project learn to *see the text*.

REFERENCES

Anne Frank House. (2013). *Anne Frank house: A museum with a story.* Amsterdam, the Netherlands: Anne Frank Stichting.

Britzman, D. (1998). *Lost subject, contested objects: Toward a psychoanalytic inquiry of learning.* New York, NY: SUNY Press.

Britzman, D. (1999). "Dimensions of a lonely discovery": Anne Frank and the question of pedagogy. In J. P. Robertson, (Ed.), *Teaching for a tolerant world, grades K-6: Essays and resources* (pp. 294–312). Urbana, IL: National Council of Teachers of English.

Cahnmann-Taylor, M., & Souto-Manning, M. (2010). *Teachers act up! Creating multicultural learning communities through theatre.* New York, NY: Teachers College Press.

Claxton, G. (2015). *Intelligence in the flesh: Why your mind needs your body much more than it thinks.* New Haven, CT: Yale University Press.

Edmiston, B. (2014). *Transforming teaching and learning with active and dramatic approaches: Engaging students across the curriculum.* New York, NY: Routledge.

Eisner, E. (2002). *The enlightened eye: Qualitative inquiry and the enhancement of educational practice.* New York, NY: Macmillan.

Frank, A. (1952). *The diary of a young girl.* New York, NY: Bantam.

Freire, P. (1970). *Pedagogy of the oppressed.* New York, NY: Continuum.

Gray, M. (2015). *Teaching the Holocaust: Practical approaches for ages 11–18.* New York, NY: Routledge.

Groenke, S. L., Maples, J., & Henderson, J. (2010). Raising "hot topics" through young adult literature. *Voices from the Middle, 17*(4), 29–36.

Harste, J. C. (2014). The art of learning to be critically literate. *Language Arts, 92*(2), 90–102.

Janks, H. (2009). *Literacy and power.* New York, NY: Routledge.

Jones, S. (2006). Lessons from Dorothy Allison: Teacher education, social class, and critical literacy. *Changing English, 13*(3), 293–305.

Juzwik, M. M. (2013). The ethics of teaching disturbing pasts: Reader response, historical contextualization, and rhetorical (con)textualization of Holocaust texts in English. *English Education, 45*(3), 284–309.

Kress, G., & van Leeuwen, T. (2001). *Multimodal discourse.* London, UK: Arnold.

LaCapra, D. (1994). *Representing the Holocaust: History, theory, trauma.* Ithaca, NY: Cornell University Press.

Landay, E., & Wootton, K. (2012). *A reason to read: Linking literacy and the arts.* Cambridge, MA: Harvard Education Press.

Lewis, C. (2000). Critical issues: Limits of identification: The personal, pleasurable and critical in reader response. *Journal of Literacy Research, 32*(2), 253–266.

Lewis, C., & Crampton, A. (2016). Emotion as mediated action in doing research on learning. In M. Zembylas & P. A. Schultz, (Eds.), *Methodological advances in research on emotion and education* (pp. 137–150). New York, NY: Springer Publishing.

Magilow, D. H., & Silverman, L. (2015). *Holocaust representations in history: An introduction.* New York, NY: Bloomsbury.

National Council of Teachers of English Position Statement. (2012). *The students' right to read.* Retrieved from www.ncte.org/positions/statements/righttoreadguideline.

Prose, F. (2009). *Anne Frank: The book, the life, the afterlife.* New York, NY: Harper Collins.

Ritchie, S. (2017). Extension: Innocence, intersectionality and normativity: Choosing powerful picturebooks about gender diversity. In R. J. Meyer & K. F. Whitmore (Eds.), *Reclaiming early childhood literacies: Narratives of hope, power and vision* (pp. 60–63). New York, NY: Routledge.

Rosenblatt, L. (1978). *The reader, the text, the poem: The transactional theory of the literary work.* Carbondale: Southern Illinois University Press.

Rubin, J. E. (2000). *Teaching about the Holocaust through drama.* Charlottesville, VA: New Plays.

Schweber, S. (2004). *Making sense of the Holocaust: Lessons from classroom practice.* New York, NY: Teachers College Press.

Shandler, J. (2012). From diary to book: Text, object, structure. In B. K. Kirshenblatt-Gimblett & J. Shandler (Eds.), *Anne Frank unbound: Media, imagination, memory* (pp. 25–58). Bloomington: Indiana University Press.

Shawn, K. (1995). Current issues in Holocaust education. *Dimensions: A journal of Holocaust studies, 9*(2), 15–18.

Siegel, M. (1995). More than words: The generative power of transmediation for learning. *Canadian Journal of Education, 20*(4), 455–475.

Spector, K., & Jones, S. (2007). Constructing Anne Frank: Critical literacy and the Holocaust in eighth-grade English. *Journal of Adolescent and Adult Literacy, 51*(1), 36–48.

Stein, P. (2008). Multimodal instructional practices. In J. Coiro, M. Knobel, C. Lankshear, & D. J. Leu (Eds.), *Handbook of research on new literacies* (pp. 871–898). New York, NY: Erlbaum.

Suhor, C. (1984). Toward a semiotics-based curriculum. *Journal of Curriculum Studies, 16*(3), 247–257.

Sumara, D. J. (2002). *Why reading literature in school still matters: Imagination, interpretation, insight.* Mahwah, NJ: Erlbaum.

Totten, S., & Feinberg, S. (Eds.). (2001). *Teaching and studying the Holocaust.* Boston, MA: Allyn & Bacon.

USHMM. (n.d.). Guidelines for teaching about the Holocaust. Retrieved from: www.ushmm.org/educators/teaching-about-the-holocaust/general-teaching-guidelines

van der Stroom, G., & Massotty, S. (Eds.). (2010). *Anne Frank's tales from the secret annexe.* London, UK: Halban Publishers.

Woodcock, C., & Hakeem, P. (2015). "The power of our words and flesh": An experienced literacy coach's love letter to incoming educators about the transformational roles of relationships and the body in learning. *Journal of Language and Literacy Education, 11*(1), 13–33.

Zapruder, A. (Ed.). (2002). *Salvaged pages: Young writers' diaries of the Holocaust.* New Haven, CT: Yale University Press.

Zembylas, M. (2014). Theorizing "difficult knowledge" in the aftermath of the "affective turn": Implications for curriculum and pedagogy in handling traumatic representations. *Curriculum Inquiry, 44*(3), 390–412.

Chapter 2
Seeing the Text

FIGURE 2.1 Three of the four parts to Ellsworth Kelly's "Memorial," on permanent display at the United States Holocaust Memorial Museum

Photo: Edward Owen.

Fred Whittaker leads his eighth-grade students on an annual trip to the United States Holocaust Memorial Museum (USHMM) in Washington, DC. The class spends time in two reflection-evoking spaces: the third-floor lounge, where an art installation called "Memorial" (see Figure 2.1) invites visitors to face a wall sculpture below windows of natural light, and the Hall of Remembrance, where an eternal flame burns.

Before visitors leave the museum, they read a passage from the Book of Deuteronomy inscribed above the flame:

> Only guard yourself and guard your soul carefully, lest you forget the things your eyes saw, and lest these things depart your heart all the days of your life. And you shall make them known to your children, and to your children's children.

This year, Holocaust survivor Fred Gross accompanies the class on the trip. Mr. Gross shares his story with the class in the USHMM's Hall of Remembrance.

Upon return from their trip and back in the classroom, as part of the debriefing of their experiences, Fred asks the students to focus on the third-floor lounge and the Hall of Remembrance.

Lisa speaks up first. She says, "The [third-floor lounge] isn't white, it's a very well-lit room with blank painting canvases; the blank canvases told the stories."

"You're populating those spaces with your memories," Fred agrees. "You're bringing people to life. In the Hall of Remembrance, this is where emotion could come back. It felt wrong to cry and wrong to laugh anywhere else in the USHMM. In the Hall of Remembrance, though, you could show any emotion (*he laughs*) and show (*his voice cracks*) sadness. Having joy and laughter honors the Holocaust and its victims."

Vanessa adds, "And it helps us to remember how they had joy, laughter, and tears, too."

Danielle says, "You can paint stories. When we heard Mr. Gross's story, you could see the paintings come alive. We're called to paint those faces and those stories every day in our lives."

Robin says, "It almost felt wrong to look at the blank picture frames. I felt a longing for something to be there. There was an absence in that place."

Fred listens, then adds some background information for the class. "The United States Holocaust Memorial Museum consciously uses light and dark throughout the building. When there is lots of stuff to look at, the place is very dark. When there is nothing to look at—as in the white room [the third-floor lounge]—it is extraordinarily bright. The blank canvases in the white room are called portraits. What's missing?" he asks, and then answers his own question as he shares a more personal response. "People. Yet, I can't help but continue to look at the portraits. An odd longing comes over me, gathered around the essence of missing, absence."

As Fred and his students reflect on their experiences in the USHMM, their visceral responses in that space are interpretations of "the things [their] eyes saw." Fred and his students orchestrate this narrative by weaving each other's language and imagery into each reflective response. Lisa makes a rich interpretation of the blank canvases, which tell the stories not only of the victims of the Holocaust, but also of all of the stories that would never be told by the descendants of those victims. (Indeed, the artist compares these canvases with memorial tablets upon which are listed anonymously all of the names of Holocaust victims [USHMM, Memorial by Ellsworth Kelly]). Fred builds on this idea by suggesting that imagining the image brings people to life and that it's appropriate to respond with emotion to the men and women who lived and died during the Holocaust. Vanessa reminds the collective group about the responsibility of memory: "It helps us to remember how they had joy, laughter, and tears, too." Danielle then makes a connection to everyday life and how students are responsible for painting the stories of the blank canvases each and every day, echoing Fred's earlier comment about "bringing people to life." Robin responds to the blank canvases by reflecting on the emotional response to the absence of images—it doesn't feel right to look at blank paintings, and she longs for something, anything to be there. Fred provides some contextual information to support Robin's comment and prompt further reflection about the questions that the USHMM provokes. In his response, he uses his students' language to synthesize the conversation to that point ("blank ... canvases" noted by Lisa and "longing" and "absence" named by Robin).

In this chapter, we consider how students and their teachers transact with visual images as part of their interpretations of challenging texts. As we described in Chapter 1, we are interested in the embodied and emotional work involved in configuring linguistic and visual meanings and we think about this as "layering literacies." Although most students aren't able to travel to the USHMM like Fred's students do annually, teachers can engage all students with nonlinguistic texts. Visual texts are particularly evocative because they open up "multiple meanings that are determined not only by the artists but also the viewer and the context of viewing (both the immediate circumstance and the larger sociohistorical context)" (Leavy, 2015, p. 224).

Educators increasingly recognize the value of visual texts in teaching and learning about English Language Arts content. From visual depictions of settings described in novels, to advertisements that teachers and students critically deconstruct, to graphic novels that integrate visual elements in the narrative structure of the genre, visual texts do not merely complement linguistic texts. Visual texts exist in a dialectical relationship with linguistic texts. This means visual texts shape the meanings of linguistic texts and are shaped by them (Serafini, 2014).

Visual texts provide alternative access points to the curriculum for all learners, and particularly for those whose strengths extend beyond the linguistic mode, such as learners working to read grade-appropriate texts, learners who are becoming literate in a new language, and many others. Understanding how and why visual literacies inform learning about challenging texts is central to our developing pedagogical theory and practice.

MAKING MEANING THROUGH IMAGE

In this chapter, we describe three visual arts-related instructional strategies designed to bring learners closer to a variety of challenging Holocaust texts, to the context of *The Diary*, and to each other. Cordel, Icons, and Archives are learning experiences that engage students with visual texts to represent, read, create, recreate, and, ultimately, deepen meaning. We find these strategies to be especially powerful in facilitating learning about challenging texts because they disrupt the verbocentric mode of learning typically privileged in U.S. classrooms, and encourage the type of risk-taking we think is necessary in learning deeply about subject matter related to the Holocaust.

We present the visual strategies in a purposeful sequence; we begin with the strategy that is most directly and narrowly prepared by teachers (Cordel) and end with the strategy that is most explicitly student driven (Archives). In doing so, we provide a scaffold for you and other teachers to take increasing pedagogical risks while infusing the visual arts into classroom pedagogies of practice. Throughout our descriptions, we consider how *seeing the text* is a fundamental component of layering literacies.

Teacher Voice Box

It was a risk almost every day, but I don't want to say that to discourage anyone. I kind of think that it's fun to take those risks and to push it and to make people think. And, you know, there were some pieces in the show that we did that were controversial, but I think it's okay. If you want social justice, social reform, or to make people think, sometimes you have to push the envelope. And so risk-taking takes place all along, all the steps of the way.

Kim Joiner, drama teacher

Teacher Voice Box

If you don't have a teaching whiplash on occasion—hopefully more frequently—you are not changing or evolving or accessing newness yourself. Break my world apart sometimes, and then I always have fresher eyes. And I'm really glad that it happened...

Fred Whittaker, science and religion teacher

Seeing from a Different Perspective: Cordel

Although visual iconography from the Holocaust exists in abundance and often reflects immediately the enormity of the catastrophe (e.g. crematoria, train cars with skeletal bodies, children peering from behind concentration camp fences), we don't recommend inundating students with such devastating images, especially when introducing the topic. Remember Fred Whittaker's suggestion that "Before students can understand the six million number, they have to understand the number one." Introducing the Holocaust through devastating images can result in students quickly distancing themselves from those who perpetrated, assisted, and stood by while others succumbed to, suffered through, and actively fought against genocide.

Cordel is used to invite students to take a closer look at the lives of those who *lived* during the Holocaust. Called Literatura de Cordel, or "string literature" (Landay & Wootton, 2012, p. 36), cordels originated in northeastern Brazil where they display stories and poems on street corners and market places, usually as a way of displaying them for sale. Simply by attaching a cord or rope between two poles or hanging points in a classroom, the multi-functional cordel reconstitutes where and how texts are engaged. And just as it functioned for Brazilian artists, students may engage in diverse ways with various visual and linguistic texts that are suspended from it.

Drama teacher Kim Joiner hangs excerpts from Anne's diary alongside information about historical events, propaganda posters, and maps of nations' borders from the period. These texts are interspersed with poems from children, adolescents, and adults who wrote about their experiences during the Second World War. Strategic juxtapositions of texts like these provide and provoke storytelling opportunities for both teachers and students. Kim and her drama students use the cordel in a number of different ways as they answer their essential question (Wiggins & McTighe, 2005): "What is your humanity footprint?" The cordel serves as the visual and symbolic center of their study of *The Diary*.

Kim is fortunate that her drama classroom is a wide-open space; chairs for the students ring the perimeter. Kim and her dad fashioned her cordel with a clothesline strung between two wooden poles and it is often stretched down one long wall in front of a smart board. It is not unusual for students to first approach the cordel with curiosity and lots of chatter as standing up and moving in the classroom is, unfortunately, an unusual practice for most students and teachers. Initial energy transforms into quiet intensity though, as students encounter the cordel with each other, physically standing side-by-side. To prepare for such an experience, teachers invite students to take time as they approach the cordel and seek out a text that they would like to work with in greater depth. Each student searches for a text that speaks to him or her specifically. Figures 2.2 through 2.4 show one student crouching down in front of the cordel to get a better view, eighth-graders' intensive gazes, and one teacher's embodied emotional reaction to different Holocaust-related texts.

As learners slowly move from one artifact to another, they begin to read more carefully the visual and print texts in relative silence. Learners speak in hushed tones in reverence before the stories of the lives they encounter. Sometimes learners lean forward to get a closer look at a small detail or move back to allow space for someone else to view the texts. Their bodies work in harmony as they become more keenly aware of each other, and they position themselves along

FIGURE 2.2 A cordel with multimodal texts in Kim Joiner's classroom
Photo: Ashley L. Shelton Arnold.

FIGURE 2.3 Students enter the text by browsing the cordel in Kim Joiner's classroom
Photo: Ashley L. Shelton Arnold.

FIGURE 2.4 Teachers respond to the challenging texts presented on the cordel
Photo: Kathryn F. Whitmore.

the cordel in a way that allows everyone to be included in a shared experience. It is as if together they can better encounter and interrogate the realities and reflections depicted on the papers in front of them.

Eighth-grade English Language Arts teacher Kelly Holland invites her 110 eighth-grade students to work with the cordel as they initiate their study of *The Diary* and the Holocaust. Kelly introduces her students to the study with the essential question: What does it mean to bear witness to the suffering of others? Although we do suggest that photographs be introduced sparingly and intentionally, especially when beginning a study of the Holocaust, we also recognize how each classroom is a sociocultural context in which teachers ultimately know their students best and make instructional decisions in their best interests. Not unlike the teacher in Schweber's (2004) study who found a way to simulate activities in non-trivial ways that supported students' sense-making, Kelly carefully crafts this Cordel activity and calls attention to the emotional and psychological devastation that accompanied the physical torture endured by millions.

Kelly suspends 34 large black and white photographs on a cordel across the center of her classroom so that images are available on both sides of the line, as shown in Figure 2.5. Her decision means students confront the visual texts and each other as they enter and engage with the challenging content. The photographs depict life in the Jewish Ghetto of Łódź and various death camps. After a generative and extended discussion about words that exist in our society that relate to discrimination, Kelly asks her students to engage with the photographs on the cordel. Students silently examine the photographs and the silence promotes "thick air"—a solemn atmosphere conducive to storytelling that we further explore in Chapter 4—to contextualize their learning of visual content.

FIGURE 2.5 Kelly Holland's students move quietly through the cordel as their study begins
Photo: Ashley L. Shelton Arnold.

Next, students write three discrimination-related words associated with the Holocaust on sticky notes and attach them to the photographs (see Figure 2.6; USHMM, Washing and shaving). They spend a few minutes writing in their journals about the concept of discrimination before Kelly leads a discussion about the relationships between the words and the images.

Students post words like "humiliation," "not-human," and "abuse" all over a graphic image of Jews being stripped of their clothing. Adam explains, "They're bathing them like animals."

"What else are they taking?" asks Kelly.

Devin offers, "Dignity."

"What is dignity?" Kelly asks.

"[A] sense of self pride," Devin responds. Other students note that the individuals in the photographs have no hair, recognizing that "They'll all look the same," and, emphasizing the symbolic meaning of hair: "It makes me, me."

We developed a multimodal assessment tool we call the Visual Learning Analysis (VLA) to invite student and teacher reflections about their learning. The VLA prompts learners to closely examine photographs of classroom action for the nonlinguistic ways in which learning takes place through gaze, gesture, posture, and proximity. Figure 2.7 provides detailed procedures for using the VLA in your classroom.

FIGURE 2.6 An example of a photograph labeled with words of discrimination
Photo: James S. Chisholm.

Visual Learning Analysis

LEVEL I

Spread printed color photographs on a large table. Students look at them collectively.

Ask: What do you see here? How are learners' bodies making meaning? What are teachers'

bodies doing?

LEVEL II

Students select one photograph each that is particularly indicative of themes to understand more

clearly, such as empathy, movement, and risk-taking.

Students tape these photographs onto legal-size blank paper and draw and write on them to label

what is evident at a micro-image level.

Direct students through the following series of prompts:

Eyes. Notice the eyes of each person in the photo. Who or what are they looking at? Who is

looking away? What are the expressions of the eyes communicating?

Hands. Where are the hands of key players? What do gestures convey?

Posture. What meanings do bodies convey? Who leans toward others? Who leans away?

Positioning and proximity. How are bodies positioned in the space? Who is close to whom? Who

is separated?

LEVEL III

Use the essential questions from the curriculum to prompt a deeper, more specific analysis.

LEVEL IV

Students share their individual analyses with the group.

FIGURE 2.7 Procedures for the Visual Learning Analysis (VLA)

There are four levels that make up the procedures we use during the VLA. During Level I, we invite groups of four to five students to broadly examine sets of color photographs of students engaged in arts-based learning activities. Asking the group to look collectively at the photographs, we ask: What do you see here? How are learners' bodies making meaning? What are teachers' bodies doing? In Level II, students select one image for a closer look. Prompts focus their attention on the nonlinguistic ways in which learning takes place:

- Eyes. Notice the eyes of each person in the photo. Who or what are they looking at? Who is looking away? What are the expressions of the eyes communicating?

- Hands. Where are the hands of key players positioned? What do gestures convey?
- Posture. What meanings do bodies convey? Who leans toward others? Who leans away?
- Positioning and proximity. How are bodies positioned in the space? Who is close to whom? Who is separated?

Specific inquiry questions guide Level III of the VLA. For our study, we focused our attention on:

- Risk-taking: How do you see risk-taking happening [or not] in the photo?
- Movement: In what ways does movement contribute to meaning making?
- Empathy: How do students and the teacher demonstrate and explore an understanding of empathy?

Students mark their responses to these prompts directly onto and/or around the photographs. Finally, during Level IV, students share their individual analyses with the group. We record and transcribe these conversations and use them to further understand the meanings generated throughout the process.

Figure 2.8 is an example of a VLA about the Cordel strategy. Callie writes about how focused her classmates are in the photograph and how it reflects their interest in the topic as they explore the cordel for the first time. Callie writes the following words on and around the photo: community, serious, concentrating, still, quiet, focus, standing, watching, reading, close, crossed arms, hands in pockets, tense, togetherness, taking in, interested, wanting to learn, legs apart, looking at Anne's picture, serious expressions, tough information. Callie's reflection demonstrates the solemnity with which students approach the cordel, the seriousness with which they encounter the multimodal texts, and her appreciation for the body's capacity to reflect these emotions and intellectual expressions.

Delilah and Yasmine select the same photo as Callie in Figure 2.8 to complete their VLAs. Delilah notes on her VLA, "Students are somewhat isolated, as if this is a private experience." In the white space to the right side of the photo, Yasmine writes: "[P]eople were actually reading the cordel, and paying attention to what the pieces on it actually said. Instead of just skimming, they are intently reading so they can get a good understanding of the topic." We agree with Yasmine's assertion that she and her classmates are, indeed, "actually reading," "paying attention," and "intently reading."

In fact, the differences between reading these texts in desks and reading them while standing and moving is striking. Cordel provokes, in this instance, a solitude and seriousness, as well as an extended commitment to the reading that could not likely be anticipated by distributing to students a physical stack of figuratively heavy and print centric texts.

Cordel affords classrooms different possibilities with which to encounter texts (collaboratively and personally), different perspectives from which to engage texts (standing, moving, returning to), and different types of texts to juxtapose in meaningful ways (children's poetry next to expository texts that detail the conditions inside concentration camps). It is a still and solemn experience with which students approach their study of *The Diary* and the Holocaust. Slow and deliberate movements and the proximity of bodies to each other and multimodal texts, as well as the invisible bonding that occurs during the close examination of artifacts, immerse students in the world of Anne Frank.

FIGURE 2.8 Callie's Visual Learning Analysis (VLA) describes her reading of bodies and visual texts at the cordel
Photo: Ashley L. Shelton Arnold.

Seeing the Abstract: Icons

Aprill and Wootton (n.d.) describe the visual arts instructional strategy called Icons developed by artist Bernard Williams in his work with Chicago Public Schools. Williams introduces students to the power of Icons by inviting them to discuss a subject and distill that subject into a list of words. Students select one word to represent visually using only scissors and paper. Aprill and Wootton (n.d.) suggest that the power of this learning tool can be explained by the technical simplicity of the art-making, the relative inexpensive cost for materials, the amplification of voices from the individual and the collective group of learners (when individual icons are placed among other icons), and the recasting of meaning from linguistic and abstract concepts to visual and concrete images. As learners create these visual texts, they layer understandings and literacies and inform and activate their subsequent engagement with the subject they are undertaking.

Kim uses Icons early in her class's study to help her drama students "see" the text of *The Diary*. The students discuss Anne's experiences in the annex and generate a list of words related to imagery and emotion. They write one word each on slips of paper and place the papers in a bowl; a long list of words is generated that includes: innocent, tenacious, courage, inspire, loving, encouraging, hope, and many more. Next, individual students select one word from the bowl to represent with an icon.

The students use only scissors, glue, and tan and black construction paper to create these visual representations. Kim encourages them to work independently, with partners, or in small groups (see Figure 2.9). As the students finish these images, they hang them on the cordel. In the next few days they will serve as a backdrop when students perform dramatizations about them.

We follow Brittany through the Icon process. She selects the word "scared" from the bowl of choices and sits with a group of classmates on the floor to make art. Her representation of scared is at once beautiful and haunting as it hangs on the cordel (see Figure 2.10). It appears to be a creature with tendrils that flow behind and around it, even extending beyond the frame of the paper. Much smaller, a body sits upright in a bed in the right bottom corner. The creature's spooky long arm, with several bony extending fingers, reaches toward the child-like body.

FIGURE 2.9 Students in Kim Joiner's class work to create their icons
Photo: Irina V. McGrath.

FIGURE 2.10 Brittany's icon of the word "scared" hangs on the cordel in Kim Joiner's classroom

Photo: Irina V. McGrath.

As learners move across linguistic and visual modes, and discuss various ways of re-presenting concepts across sign systems, they generate new insights. The "scared" icon, as a specific example, represents powerfully and visually the abstract terror that hung over the heads of Anne and the other seven people with whom she hid from the Nazis in the annex. The image also represents in the relative size and position of the figures in the frame, the omnipresence and omnipotence of the source of fear: the overwhelming and ominous sense of the creature in contrast to the seemingly bewildered and small child. Finally, by placing the monster's fingers as close to the child-like figure as possible, but without touching the figure on the bed, Brittany offers a reading of "scared" that reflects the emotions Anne expressed in her diary: on any given day someone might betray their trust and turn them and their helpers in to the Gestapo. (We return to "scared" in Chapter 3 when we describe how Kim continues to engage students in the Icon experience by using Tableau.)

Layering these interpretations of the text through visual icons promotes learners' concretization of concepts and creates a new text with which readers transact. Figure 2.11 is a collage of icons from other students in Kim's class. These images are reflections of the many attributes of Anne—each of which taken out of context and standing alone would be misrepresentative and even dangerous as a single characterization. Anne was determined *and* innocent as she faced

FIGURE 2.11 Icons from students in Kim Joiner's class (left to right, top to bottom): "determined," "innocent," "ambition," "optimistic"

Photo: James S. Chisholm.

adversity. She was ambitious *and* scared. Thus, like her readers of today, Anne was a complex teenager—part of her appeal and a point of connection. When the icons are strung together on the cordel, the more accurate and complex Anne is visible, helping students see "the one" so they can connect to the six million.

Kim and the students repurpose the icons at the end of the study. Kim moves the cordel to the space where audience members wait to enter the theater to see the students' final performances related to their work with *The Diary*. Hanging from the cordel, the icons become a visual and public invitation to the audience to imagine what they mean and what they convey about the Anne Frank and Holocaust performances they are about to see.

Seeing Life: Archives

Harste (2014) argues, specifically, for the value of the arts to promote *abduction*, rather than deduction or induction, noting that "the exploration of possibility, creativity, and imagination" is "the only form of logic that allows newness into the system" (p. 97). In working through challenging texts related to the Holocaust, for which "understandings" through deduction or induction are potentially less useful than questions arrived at through critical perspective taking, abduction represents a particularly compelling logic of inquiry.

The instructional strategy Archives, as taught by Fred Whittaker, is an example of the power of abduction—"the jumping to conclusions intuitively without an explicit set of arguments to follow" (Harste, 2014, p. 97)—and its relationship to agency. Fred and his students address the following question during their study of *The Diary* and the Holocaust, "As we bear witness to a world in which people are marginalized, forgotten and persecuted, what obligations to social justice does our faith place upon us?" Fred is well known in the Louisville community for his annual study of the Holocaust. As indicated in this chapter's opening vignette, every year the study includes an eighth-grade trip to the USHMM.

Long before their trip to Washington, DC, however, Fred is thoughtful about introducing his students to the challenging content and context of the Holocaust, and Archives is one of his key strategies. The image in Figure 2.12 depicts the large bulletin board in the hallway outside of Fred's classroom when Archives is complete. The center of the display reproduces an excerpt from the Book of Isaiah (43:10): "You are my witnesses"—the same passage that graces the central hall of the USHMM. From a distance, the iconic yellow stars call out to viewers with an immediate visual reference to the Holocaust.

On closer look, the bulletin board features dozens of smaller poignant photographs of eighth graders paired with historical snapshots of ordinary people from the USHMM archive. The eighth graders and the individuals from decades ago are in mirrored positions, doing ordinary recreational activities, sharing family dinners, and accomplishing daily life. Fred reminds us that he never mentions "the six million number" (referring to the number of Jews who were killed by Nazis) when introducing students to the Holocaust. "It makes it too easy to *other* them," he says. "I want [students] to fall in love with them, not to feel sorry for them. Or both."

FIGURE 2.12 A large bulletin board outside Fred Whittaker's classroom is filled with archives—
images of the students and people who lived during the Holocaust
Photo: James S. Chisholm.

Fred encourages students to reflect on the activities they enjoy (e.g. reading, digging in the sand, riding bikes, etc.), then provides them with the web address for the USHMM photographic archives site. Students search the archives to find photographs that depict similar activities and select three photos from their own family albums in which they are engaging in similar activities. Fred challenges students to select the image sets that "match" most closely in terms of posture, expression, and gesture.

In the photo in Figure 2.13, two adolescents pose proudly with a snowman. This picture is juxtaposed with a black-and-white image from the USHMM archive in which a similar-looking snowman and background connect the persons in both images. The archive depicts the Starkopf family *ca.* 1945–1946, who ultimately immigrated to the United States, in the Feldafing displaced person camp (USHMM, The Starkopf family). Students draw on different motivations as they select Archive images (e.g. similar poses and contexts) and conceptualize the meanings of these juxtapositions in their own lives (e.g. related interests). In a typical reflection, Lawrence notes,

I found a picture of me building a snowman and then I went on the website and found images of other kids from the Holocaust building snowmen and there was so many and there was like a perfect one where it was like the exact same pose and it was like, 'Wow!' This, like, was directly related.

FIGURE 2.13 Building snowmen across time and space
Photo: James S. Chisholm.

FIGURE 2.14 Children playing with sand buckets on the beach in two times, places, and circumstances

Photo: James S. Chisholm.

Photographs of two children playing with pails and shovels in sand on a beach (Figure 2.14; USHMM, Manny Mandel) and horseback riding surrounded by nature (Figure 2.15; USHMM, Chagit Elster) remind students that their current interests were also the interests of (at least) one of the millions of people whom the Nazis targeted to murder. These are everyday scenes of those who lived during the Holocaust. The photographs humanize people who are not only historically and geographically distant, but, for many learners in U.S. middle schools, also linguistically and culturally different. The images help to recognize and begin to close the gap between self and other for students of the Holocaust.

Yet, students move beyond their initial reflections about physical similarities and common leisurely interests, too. After Arianna marks the similarities in the images she juxtaposes in Figure 2.15, she contemplates the meanings of the connections she is making to the past:

Like me, [she] had brown, wavy, curly hair and the horse was facing the same direction and I don't....even though it may seem kind of freaky, I don't think it's a coincidence. Like I feel like we've learned so much about our Holocaust victims and how we've like, I guess, taken them in, I guess.

The photo depicts "Chagit Elster, a member of the Hashomer Hatzair Zionist collective, [riding] the only horse on their farm in Zarki" *ca.* 1941–1942 (USHMM, Chagit Elster). Arianna articulates an emotional, spiritual resonance that characterizes her selection process from the archives ("I don't think it's a coincidence"), uses the collective and possessive pronoun ("our") to mark her relationship toward the women and men whose lives she is studying, and internalizes their stories ("taken them in") into her own.

FIGURE 2.15 Arianna and Chagit ride horseback in nature, making connections across time
and space
Photo: James S. Chisholm.

In addition to identifying similar and unique activities, poses, and interests, students also
select archive photos for their everyday, spontaneous, non-specific nature, and the *living* that
such activity portrays. As Beth notes with regard to a pair of photographs she selects:

> Well I chose my picture because the way I'm doing it, it wasn't an intentional picture that
> was taken. She wasn't posing for it like I wasn't and so I just thought it was… I liked the
> way they both fit together because like we weren't doing anything special like we weren't
> like playing soccer, we were just living…

Finally, some students, like Liam, use Archives to imagine inhabiting the thoughts and feelings
of the people depicted in the archive images. Liam describes to James his selection process for the
image in Figure 2.16, of Liebke (Leon) Shlanski in 1940 in Eisiskes (USHMM, A Jewish child).

Liam says, "Like, it wasn't going to be poses [i.e. impromptu, not staged]. It was what was on
our minds at the same time. So I have a snowboard and the other guy has skis. But we were both
having fun and we both wanted to get down the hill. Which I can't do and it was more like I
wanted to think what was going on in that moment for him and what was going on in that moment for me and who was taking the picture. That had something to do with it."

"And how did that make you feel?" asks James.

FIGURE 2.16 "I wanted to think what was going on in that moment for him"
Photo: James S. Chisholm.

"It made me feel more connected to the time zone," answers Liam, "because it made me feel like I could be in that picture because we're both thinking the same thing, we both are the same age in that picture … on those lines … it could merge."

Although these eighth graders can't literally time and space travel, this activity allows them to think deeply about—even inhabit, if temporarily—distant places temporally and spatially. Tara expresses this phenomenon perfectly when asked when she felt most connected to Anne Frank during the unit, and what made her feel that way. She writes, "I felt most connected when we started learning facts and seeing pictures of the situation. It made me feel this way because I felt that I could sort of feel or connect with her (not exactly)." With her parenthetical expression of the reality of "not exactly" knowing Anne or the other individuals, Tara indicates her understanding that she still doesn't really know Anne Frank. Her words teach us that layering literacies with visual strategies like Archives supports students' complex thinking and nuanced understanding that although they come to know much about Anne and her life, they can't "exactly."

The single collective image that results from Archives, composed of the many individual juxtaposed images, creates continuity across time and space and promotes students' relational construction of knowledge. In this way, students metaphorically place themselves into the lives of

Holocaust victims, survivors, and their families. They connect to individual lives in single images before they encounter the enormity of the number of lives and families who were devastated by the Holocaust. As Liam comments, "It made me feel more connected to the time … [be]cause it made me feel like I could be in that picture because we're both thinking the same thing, we both are the same age in that picture." This connection helps students see the individual life within the context of the six million deaths. From that point, students are positioned well to pose authentic and critical questions about what it means to bear witness to Anne Frank in the 21st century.

LAYERING VISUAL LITERACIES

The visual arts expand ways of knowing and the modes through which learners can perform their understandings of the curriculum. Seeing the text encourages students to take up new perspectives that (a) promote physically different, meaningful, and collaborative reading experiences with Cordel; (b) move across sign systems, generate new meanings about important textual themes, and make concrete otherwise abstract concepts with Icons; and (c) juxtapose images from their own family photo albums with Jewish families in the first half of the 20th century, resulting in students' relational and historical learning about individual lives before, during, and after the Holocaust with Archives. In each of these visual literacies strategies, students read and construct abstract concepts through the visual mode. They create and interpret challenging visual texts as they layer potential meanings for linguistic texts.

These classroom events illustrate the power of seeing challenging texts—in this case as related to the Holocaust. In Chapter 3, we turn from students *seeing* the text to students *being* the text. We explore how embodied literacies is another layer that adds depth to students' transactions with challenging texts.

REFERENCES

Aprill, A., & Wootton, K. (n.d.). Icons. *Habla best practice handbook 2010*. Merida, Mexico: Habla: El Centro de Lengua y Cultura. Retrieved from: http://habla.org/pdf_handbook/icons.pdf.

Harste, J. C. (2014). The art of learning to be critically literate. *Language Arts, 92*(2), 90–102.

Landay, E., & Wootton, K. (2012). *A reason to read: Linking literacy and the arts*. Cambridge, MA: Harvard Education Press.

Leavy, P. (2015). *Method meets art: Arts-based research practice* (2nd ed.). New York, NY: The Guilford Press.

Schweber, S. (2004). *Making sense of the Holocaust: Lessons from classroom practice*. New York, NY: Teachers College Press.

Serafini, F. (2014). *Reading the visual: An introduction to multimodal literacy*. New York, NY: Teachers College Press.

United States Holocaust Memorial Museum (USHMM). (n.d.). A Jewish child poses on skis on a snow-covered street in Eisiskes. Retrieved from: http://collections.ushmm.org/search/catalog/pa1127095.

USHMM. (n.d.). Chagit Elster, a member of the Hashomer Hatzair Zionist collective, rides the only horse on their farm in Zarki. Retrieved from: http://collections.ushmm.org/search/catalog/pa1060218.

USHMM. (n.d.). Manny Mandel plays on the beach with his toys in Crikvenica on the Dalmatian coast. Retrieved from: http://collections.ushmm.org/search/catalog/pa1166067.

USHMM. (n.d.). The Starkopf family poses by a snowman in the Feldafing displaced persons camp. Retrieved from: http://collections.ushmm.org/search/catalog/pa1151787.

USHMM. (n.d.). Washing and shaving newly arrived Polish prisoners in the Buchenwald concentration camp. Retrieved from: http://collections.ushmm.org/search/catalog/pa12314.

Wiggins, G., & McTighe, J. (2005). *Understanding by design.* (2nd ed.). Alexandria, VA: Association for Supervision and Curriculum Development.

Chapter 3
Being the Text

"And the prince and the princess lived happily ever after," Amanda gestures closing the book, and says, "Goodnight, Kaeli. Sweet dreams."

Kaeli answers, "Goodnight, Mom." She closes her eyes and lies down on the floor. From the right side of the classroom two characters charge into the space; Taylor chases Sam around while yelling, "Kaeli, come back!" One of the characters shrieks.

Kaeli screams and sits straight up in bed as her mother dashes back to the scene calling, "Kaeli, are you okay?"

"I had a really bad nightmare," Kaeli says.

"It's okay," comforts Mom as she gives her a hug.

"Scene."

Amanda, Taylor, Kaeli, and Sam perform this scene and use their bodies to become characters they generate from their reading of the linguistic and visual text, "scared." (We describe how the image is created during the visual strategy called Icons in Chapter 2.) Amanda embodies a mother who kneels by a child in bed, reading from an imagined storybook that she creates by holding her hands palms up and separated, suggesting a large book.

Figure 3.1 is a still-frame photograph of movement we originally captured in digital video just as Taylor chases Sam. The lines flowing from the creature in the icon create the concept of movement that the students pick up on when they interpret the image with drama. Three of the bodies in the photograph are moving and therefore blurred. Taylor's hair, as she portrays the creature in the dream, flows out behind her as she runs, remarkably mirroring the tendrils of the creature image in "scared."

Snowber says, "We are bodies, we do not have bodies. They are a place of deep learning, and both bodily knowledge and bodily wisdom are always available to us" (2012, p. 119, cited in Leavy, 2015, p. 153). In much the same way that the girls in the opening vignette to this chapter physically dramatize visual images created from abstract linguistic concepts, we don't merely learn through our bodies; we learn *in* our bodies. As Claxton (2015) argues, "human intelligence lives in our hands just as much as in our tongues and our brains" (p. 8). Understanding the literate potential of the body is paramount for comprehensive, compelling, and progressive developments in theory and practice for arts-infused literacies learning.

FIGURE 3.1 Amanda, Taylor, Kaeli, and Sam dramatize Brittany's "scared" icon
Video Still: James S. Chisholm.

The movements the students use to embody their conceptualizations of "scared" and other words and concepts related to Anne Frank's diary (*The Diary*) (e.g. ambition, chatty, innocent, facing adversity, determined, optimistic, and tenacious) energize their learning. As Landay and Wootton (2012) note, such classroom improvisations "bring words to life, lifting language off the one-dimensional page and reinvesting it with the three-dimensional features of voice, movement, gesture, and timing" (p. 99). Breathing new life into learning deepens students' thinking as the textual interpretations they consider become increasingly complex. The process of transmediation occurs in the vignette about dramatizing "scared," when meanings are recast across sign systems: verbal (the written word), visual (the icon), dramatic (the performed scene), and again verbal (the girls' spoken reflection to the class). Transmediation is an explanation of the power of accessing multiple ways of knowing (Siegel, 1995). Landay and Wootton (2012) suggest that revisiting a concept like "scared" through such multi-semiotic means promotes enduring understandings. Further, when students layer their understandings of *The Diary* across the expressive mediums featured in the visual and dramatic arts, they focus their initial thinking around one emotional concept. This echoes our collective pedagogical call to enter into the study of the Holocaust one person, one emotion, at a time.

MAKING MEANING THROUGH MOVEMENT

In this chapter, we explore the nature of embodiment by looking across several moments in eighth-grade classrooms during studies of Anne Frank and the Holocaust. The arts-based techniques we share emphasize the body's role in literacies learning in classrooms. We are guided in this chapter by two assumptions: (1) that engagement is a prerequisite requirement for learning, and (2) that engagement increases when bodies move (Chisholm & Whitmore, 2016; Landay & Wootton, 2012; Whitmore, 2015).

Teacher Voice Box

Everybody remembers more when you do it with your body… I think that movement lends itself to a fuller understanding from your head to your heart. You know there is that connection because your movement forces you to think about the feeling.

Kim Joiner, drama teacher

We present the "being the text" arts-based instructional strategies in order of least to most complex and from most teacher-guided to most student-oriented so that teachers' risk-taking is scaffolded with these approaches. In Tableau and Pantomime, we demonstrate how students generate layered meanings with their bodies as they perform responses to excerpts from Anne Frank's diary. In Sculpture Garden, we describe how layers thicken as students use others' bodies to shape responses to Anne's writing as well as their own diary entries. And in Dramatic and Staged Performances, we detail the embodied revision processes that reflect students' voices as they compose responses to Anne's words and other Holocaust texts.

Expressing the Text: Tableau and Pantomime

One reason Cordel (described in Chapter 2) resonates with students, in addition to its inherent visual form, is because to engage in it requires that they leave their desks and seats, use classroom space in a novel way, and stand close to one another. As you and your students become comfortable using bodies to make and be made by texts, Tableau and Pantomime are accessible and implementable embodied strategies during which increasingly complex arts-based literacies might be practiced.

Tableau

One day, in Kim Joiner's drama classroom, students' warm-up by embodying an excerpt from one of Anne Frank's diary entries with Tableau. Tableau, sometimes called a still image or a frozen picture with young learners, is a "still, silent performance that involves three-dimensional representations" (Wilson, 2003, p. 375) created with participants' bodies. Kim uses Tableau in this case to help her students read and unpack various passages from *The Diary*. To start, she asks the students to "lock arms" with a partner and talk for a minute about a diary entry they have selected. Next, two sets of pairs who worked with the same passage team up to create tableaux. Kim reminds her class to refrain from talking as they negotiate their embodied responses to the entry. Instead, she suggests, students should get into "a statuesque pose … organically." Kim reads from Anne Frank's diary entry from Wednesday, April 19, 1944:

> What could be nicer than sitting before an open window, enjoying nature, listening to the birds sing, feeling the sun on your cheeks and holding a darling boy in your arms?
>
> (Frank, 1952, p. 266)

Julia, Robin, Maddie, and Sarah work together to compose a tableau. Upon hearing the words "sun on your cheeks," Robin falls to the floor and rests her tilting chin on her fingertips. Sarah, still standing, creates a C shape with her arms, which Julia immediately mirrors. They look at each other in the eyes and move slowly toward the floor to frame a window out of which Robin can look.

Seeing everyone else on the floor, Maddie also sits down and rests her chin on her right fist. The photo in Figure 3.2 shows their final position in response to the entry. Visible behind them is the cordel, which, in this image, displays visual, literary, and expository texts related to their study.

Students' embodied responses to the Anne Frank entry can be understood as what Sipe (2002) calls performative response and what Enriquez (2016) terms body-poems. These embodied responses are unique to each small group of students who negotiate their bodies as texts during Tableau. Because students have immediate access to other tableaux in the room, they can express the text through performative gestures they co-construct with each other and in response to embodied gestures they see around the room. Wilson (2003), who investigates the value of tableaux with primary grade readers, values performative gestures like the scene of Anne in the window of the annex because they "show ideas, knowledge, and interpretation." She believes performative gesture is "both a mode of expression and a thinking action" (p. 377), especially when learners explain what they do and why.

When such performative gestures are the means through which students transact with text, their bodies become poems in Rosenblatt's (1978) sense of the word (Enriquez, 2016). Body-poems are artifacts of embodied performance in reader response and, thus, create opportunities for readers to create new kinds of interpretations for their peers and teacher. However, Enriquez (2016) notes, the relative success of body-poems depends on a number of factors, including how audience members read the body-poem, how regulated body-poems are, and the identities that each body-poem projects. And body-poems, like other poems, strike their audiences in different ways. Kim often unpacks body-poems with the text, authors, and audience members after

FIGURE 3.2 Students create a tableau for Anne Frank's diary passage from April 19, 1944
Photo: James S. Chisholm

small group tableaux. In these ways, body-poems also promote enduring understandings as their meanings transform over time and with additional transactions. When Julia, Robin, Maddie, and Sarah (or their classmates in the audience) actually feel the sun on their own cheeks or hear the birds singing in their neighborhoods and reflect on that moment, they deepen and transform their transaction with Anne's diary. As Claxton (2015) notes, "Doing and thinking are not separate faculties; they are inextricably intertwined" (p. 9).

Pantomime

In addition to the improvisational and intuitive meanings bodies perform during process drama activities, students also make intentional decisions about the configuration of their bodies in space during dramatic readings of entries from *The Diary*. One type of dramatic reading is Pantomime, in which students use their bodies to silently convey the meaning of a text to their classmates, sometimes as a narrator reads a passage.

As the Pantomime in Figure 3.3 begins, two girls enter the space: Lillian shapes her body into the peaked roof of the annex by touching her fingers above her head as Allison folds her body on the floor so her back becomes a table. Lillian directs her gaze downward toward the action. A fourth learner, Monica, reads the excerpt aloud to narrate the three performers' actions. Soon Lacy enters the scene in her stocking feet and attaches to her sweatshirt a nametag that reads "Anne." She steps into a pair of boots, then kneels at the table and pantomimes writing in a coil notebook. At the conclusion of the scene, Lacy stands and steps back out of the boots as the students say, "Scene"—the ritual that indicates to spectators that the performance is complete.

FIGURE 3.3 Students pantomime a diary passage in Kim Joiner's classroom
Photo: Kathryn F. Whitmore.

The photograph of the three ascending bodies from the floor to the roof freezes the action and creates the opportunity for us to analyze multiple perspectives regarding embodied meaning making. From one perspective, Allison, Lacy, Lillian, and Monica create a "framed silence" (Schmidt, 2009, p. 250) that heightens the audience's awareness of the most minimal movements in the scene (in this case, Lacy's gesturing writing). Framed silences create opportunities for readers and learners to reflect on what is happening in an image, in a word, or a performance in order to promote questions. Further, the scene charges audience members to consider their interpretations of the relationship between the linguistic narration that Monica reads and the gestural embodiment of the rest of the group's performance (Albers, 2006). As Edmiston (2014) notes, stepping into and out of an event frames learners' actions in particular ways that shape the message for the audience in consequential ways. At the same time, audience members assume an important spectator stance, which works to help them develop a critical perspective on the performance (Edmiston, 2011).

At the conclusion of Pantomime, Allison, Lacy, Lillian, and Monica explain it to the class. They highlight the relationship between their bodies, particularly through Lillian's gaze toward Anne Frank (Lacy), and realize that their proximity, or the closeness of their bodies to each other, creates a visual and embodied sense of safety for them as performers and for the audience. Lacy notes how she uses her body in the scene to suggest tight quarters, for example. She says, "And also it was all part of her experience; the tiny house and having just a very limited space, I thought." And Lillian, whose body becomes the annex in this scene, says that the proximity of bodies creates a sense of tight enclosure that Anne wrote about in her diary, which expresses, in addition to her gift for writing and the horrors of the historical time period, the everyday mundane details of day-to-day life in the annex. She continues:

> And I wanted to be a part of her life. Like the house was a big thing and how she was in a very small space. Like a table to write the diary on. And then her thoughts, Monica (the narrator) was like her thoughts, like acting it out. So everybody had a part of Anne Frank's life.

Calvin selects a photo of his classmates during their pantomime of Anne Frank writing in the annex for the Visual Learning Analysis (VLA; see Figure 3.4), which is facilitated by Ashley Shelton Arnold, a graduate student researcher. During the debriefing discussion, Ashley asks, "What did you guys think about their group making people into inanimate objects?"

"Well," responds Zoe, "It's not really different, because we, as drama students, we have to figure out a way to use our bodies for, sometimes we have to figure out how to use our bodies [in] ways that we normally wouldn't think of."

Calvin adds, "Especially when we don't have props, we'll do anything to make the show."

Ashley asks, "What does that do for the scene, to have to use your bodies, you know, in different ways, so maybe you don't have, like you said, you don't have props to work with?"

"It adds understanding for the audience; otherwise, they would have no idea what is going on."

"What do you think the table and the house added in that scene?" asks Ashley.

"Um," Calvin says:

> It showed that Anne is in a safe place, in a safer place than she would be otherwise, and it kind of showed like the comfort she had when she would write in her diary; she had the possessions she was used to around her at this point in time and she was in her little bubble telling what has been going on.

The roof over Anne's head. Looking down as if representing the protection provided to Anne, as the annex helped her

"Stepped into her shoes" Lacy gave an abstract and literal interpretation. As she walked into the home she put on Anne's "shoes" and her nametag. As she left she took it off. It provided an interesting way to tell the story and connect

FIGURE 3.4 Calvin's Visual Learning Analysis (VLA) text emphasizes how Lacy uses her body to connect to Anne Frank and the audience
Photo: Ashley L. Shelton Arnold.

Calvin's insight during this conversation illustrates his semiotic awareness (Towndrow, Nelson, & Yusuf, 2013)—his understanding that different sign systems (e.g. linguistic, visual, gestural, etc.) express meanings differently—and emphasizes the semiotic potential of bodies in proximity to one another to convey meanings in intentional ways. When Ashley probes Calvin to share his reading of the scene, he expresses the generative potential involved in transmediating understandings from the gestural sign system of the frozen image to the linguistic sign system of the discussion. Calvin's commentary that "Anne is in a safer place" is a linguistic interpretation of the embodied consolation that Lillian and Allison provide by framing with their bodies an intimate, comforting, and private space for "Anne."

Calvin shares:

I [chose this photograph] and I talked about how she was over in the annex where they put a roof over her head protecting her and how Lacy did the literal interpretation as she walked in the door, put on her shoes, put on her name tag and how it like provided an interesting storytelling. It's great because we can relate to Lacy … and like Lacy's portrayal of the character.

Ashley said, "You mentioned the nametag to me. Why is that important?"

"Uh, because I just thought it was really interesting when she took it off afterwards. 'I was Anne, but I am not actually Anne. I just looked into her life, I explained her life.'"

"Yeah, you guys have been stepping into some big shoes to fill in this [study] haven't you?" says Ashley. "How does that make you feel?"

Zoe joins in, "I think it's easier as drama students because you get to step into other people's (and pretend) shoes like other people might not [get to do]."

"Yeah, when you step into their shoes, what are you trying to do for your audience? What do you hope they get out of it?," Ashley follows up.

Calvin makes the point more clear. He says:

> I think we are trying to give them that connection that we are trying to find at the same time because with empathizing you usually have to try to find a connection to your life and since none of us have actually experienced or seen the Holocaust, it's very difficult even when it comes to stepping into someone else's shoes. It's like trying to find a point where you can connect the dots but if we can get that down and since we are the kids acting on stage these kids in the audience can relate to us so we can help them find that connection.

Shaping the Text: Sculpture Garden

During Sculpture Garden, learners compose responses to words, images, or themes with their bodies and in so doing become texts. In such embodied responses, students work together in pairs as sculptors and clay to mold interpretations of texts. Prior to engaging in this strategy with *The Diary*, the students in Fred Whittaker's eighth-grade science and religion classroom discuss the genre of diaries. They talk about the voice, content, tentativeness, and style of diary entry writing, and use Anne's diary as a mentor text as they keep a reflective journal of their own. On occasion, Fred collects and responds to the students' diaries. During Sculpture Garden the students use their bodies to respond to excerpts from both Anne Frank's diary and their own reflective journals. With permission from the students, Fred weaves students' anonymous journal excerpts with excerpts from Anne's actual diary. It's fascinating to us that selected entries from students' journals and Anne's diary are, on paper, often indistinguishable in voice and content.

Student Voice Box

Well I think doing all these [drama] exercises, it really like makes Anne's legacy live on more than it did if you just read the book. I mean that's great if you just read the book but this is actually reliving the book. It's not just reading it.

Arianna, eighth-grade student

In Fred's classroom in a Catholic school, students work all year toward the goal of understanding how "social justice is informed by and part of their faith." Their Holocaust study focuses on learning to bear witness to Anne Frank's story. Fred is an experienced educator about the Holocaust, but ideas of arts-based instruction are new to him, particularly learning experiences that emphasize drama and movement. Teaching artist and drama educator, Talleri McCrae becomes Fred's partner for exploring these new ideas with his students. She visits the classroom once or twice a week to demonstrate process drama strategies that Fred later takes up independently with his class.

One morning, to create a space for movement to occur, the students move all the science lab tables aside and position their chairs in a circle on the outskirts of the room. Fred asks the students to share a moment of silence to "get into that frame of mind" before beginning the activity. Students then break into two groups. Fred explains that they will use their bodies in response to spoken reflections. "Sculpting a shape with their bodies," he says, will allow them to "have that courage to be bent by how you feel." In phases, each group "performs" by creating sculptures as meanings for texts being read out loud.

Talleri facilitates the students' initial work in Sculpture Garden. She invites learners to form two circles. The students in the inner circle face outward, and those in the outer circle face inward. She directs the outer circle to be "sculptors," creating the ideas in their heads using their "clay" (their inner-circle partners). Talleri offers three options for ways the students can sculpt another person and demonstrates each option with a student volunteer. First, the sculptors can show the clay how to position themselves using their own bodies—in other words, the clay can mirror the sculptor. The second option is for sculptors to ask permission to touch their partners and, once received, shape the clay into each sculptor's idea. The third option is for the sculptors to act as puppeteers, using imaginary strings to move their clay into different positions. Finally, Talleri reminds the students to use movement, and not words, to mold their "intelligent clay."

The students begin with their hands neutrally at their sides as Talleri reads the following passage, which, although written by a student, could have been penned by Anne herself:

> The times when people are moving on, when we are changing from one place to another, those are the times when we really need to hold tight to who we really are. You can't move on if you are lost.

The sculptors mirror, or move with, or puppet their partners throughout the reading of the passage, which Talleri reads aloud multiple times, working with their clay to capture its essence. She reminds students to work with levels, and to use gaze and gesture to communicate meanings, intending they should position their bodies high or low in the vertical space, and use their eyes and their whole bodies to add intensity to the meaning they convey. "Be gentle," she says, and then adds, "I know that you are finished with your sculptures when you step away from them." In Figure 3.5 a sculptor-student, David, works with his clay, Arianna. David chooses the option to mirror, guiding Arianna's movements into the positions he intends.

As Talleri reads the passage, David makes eye contact with Arianna. He projects his gaze away from his body and grabs his chin and turns it to the right, as if looking towards a moment in the future. Arianna follows by mirroring her own gaze in that direction. She places her hand over her heart as David indicates, and mirrors her other hand with his, pointing in the same direction as their collective gaze. She raises her eyebrows, nonverbally asking David to confirm if her shape reflects his intentions and David gestures with one thumb in the air. This freezes the clay into a bodily position of looking towards the future while still holding on to one's self via the hand over the heart (see Figure 3.5).

When all the individual clay is frozen and the sculptors have stepped away, Talleri invites the sculptors and the student audience to move around the sculptures and examine all the responses. The students make a complete revolution around the circle before taking their seats once more. Talleri asks the students to respond to what they see, remarking that she noticed sculptors created quite figurative responses about a rather literal statement. As the activity repeats several times, with Talleri reading a new passage for each group, students rotate roles as sculptors, clay, and audience members. Afterwards, the students debrief the Sculpture Garden experience.

Arianna reflects about her experience, "As the clay I tried to have a personal connection with the sculptor—to really try, to the best of your abilities, to imitate what [David was] thinking." Elizabeth explains, "As the sculptor was moving my arms I could feel what she was thinking and how she wanted it to be."

FIGURE 3.5 Arianna as clay, mirroring David as sculptor, in response to a diary entry
Photo: James S. Chisholm.

Teacher Voice Box

Following the Sculpture Garden strategy, Fred tells his class:
[Sculpture Garden] calls on a very deep maturity, and so many of you rose to that, so thank you for allowing us to do that. What's cool, I noticed, was what walking around the circle called on you to do and be. Although the statues were silent, there was a great demand placed on the kind of attention you had to pay and who you had to be and become to appreciate this. Stepping away from the idea that those are your friends and into the idea that they have been affected by the feelings of others. That's a big step! And you did a really good job of going into that activity and I really liked that. It makes me think that as we step in to Anne Frank and as we step in to what she was thinking and saying, that we're going to be able to go deep.
                                                    Fred Whittaker, science and religion teacher

---

Since learning happens in the body (Claxton, 2015; Lakoff & Johnson, 1999; Woodcock, 2010), embodied literacy performances like Sculpture Garden become sites for critical textual expression and transaction. Students embodying texts create signs to be interpreted by other students who hear, see, feel, and read the bodies of their classmates to construct their own meanings and develop their own semiotic awareness (Towndrow et al., 2013). Therefore, Sculpture Garden is a powerful example of being the text that emphasizes students' exploration of Anne's diary and their own writing in nonlinguistic ways, in this case by using movement and gestures to generate new meanings. As audience members observe how others use their bodies to respond to the meanings of diary entries, students perceive their bodies as powerful texts in themselves.

Important in Sculpture Garden is the emphasis on body and movement without talking—removing language from the layers that students can access and emphasizing the nonverbal. In the following strategies, Dramatic and Staged Performances, talk is layered in meaningful ways alongside movement.

Presenting the Text: Dramatic and Staged Performances

Formal dramatic productions may challenge you and many teachers and students to move outside of your comfort zones; however, as Rubin writes, "Drama is *active*" and "dramatic activity makes the content personal and immediate" (2000, p. 1, emphasis in original). Further, performing for an audience of spectators heightens students' commitment to their learning because, as Edmiston (2014) says, "without performances a person's ideas cannot be crystallized and shared with a group or carried into possible action" (p. 47). As students make their learning available publicly for witnesses in the audience, they enact particular identities as learners, actors, and people.

Student Voice Box

I think that the process of the acting has a lot to do with it because it gets you out of the book in a way and into reality like the present instead of reading about the past.

Liam, eighth-grade student

Tiffany LaVoie's eighth-grade students' study of Anne Frank is centered in understanding the concept of empathy. The students design performances using various literary and expository texts from the Holocaust. We use the label Dramatic Performance for performances in the classroom, when other students may or may not be an audience. In Dramatic Performance the goal is process. The Dramatic Performance may only occur once, and it's likely not to require any (or very minimal) props, costumes, or sets. It may or may not develop into Staged Performance. Staged Performance, in contrast, is the development of a scene, monologue, or other performance that is rehearsed and eventually staged in front of a more formal audience, which is likely to include students from other classes, families, and perhaps community members.

In the next illustrations, we share how two small groups of students work through a well-known poetic text from the Holocaust and an excerpt from Anne Frank's diary. Both examples begin as Dramatic Performance, composed and revised in class, and later become Staged Performance when they are shared with all eighth-grade students in their school, as well as guests from the community.

"First They Came for the Socialists"

Incorporating other texts from the Holocaust helps to contextualize Anne's diary in potentially powerful ways. In Chapter 6, Renita Schmidt reviews and recommends children's and adolescent literature that pairs effectively with *The Diary*. For Tiffany and her students, drama and movement are familiar, but using drama to think deeply about a challenging text is new. Early in their study, Tiffany asks small groups of students to select a document from the cordel (described in Chapter 2) to use to develop a dramatic reading. Nellie, Oscar, Dana, and Kristin select a quotation from Martin Niemöller, a Protestant pastor who spent seven years in a concentration camp for opposing the Nazi regime. One version of the well-known quotation begins, "First they came for the Socialists, and I did not speak out—Because I was not a Socialist." The version of the poetic text that students use repeats these lines and substitutes the names of various groups targeted by the Nazis: namely, Trade Unionists and Jews. The quotation ends with the speaker's stark realization that when "they came for me—and there was no one left to speak for me."

Tiffany's students find a separate space adjacent to the classroom in which to brainstorm ways to convey with their bodies the essence of Niemöller's words. After reading the quotation, they decide to have Oscar, Dana, and Kristin recite the lines that identify the Socialists, Trade Unionists, and Jews, respectively. After each student recites her or his respective line, Nellie places her hands on the shoulders of each student and guides her or him toward the floor. Students smile and laugh and giggle through the entire first rehearsal, at the end of which Nellie utters the line, "And there was no one left to speak for me," as she falls backward to the embrace of her classmates.

A series of still-frame images (Figures 3.6 through 3.8), taken from video of the students at work, allows us to look closely and deconstruct the students' embodied dispositions. Figure 3.6 presents the students during their first rehearsal. Oscar struggles to take a serious tone as he leans forward into his text and gestures with his right hand as if pulling himself through his lines. Dana, in the center, locks herself in place and laughs at Oscar's attempt as she looks off into the distance, while Kristin smirks casually in amusement.

The students rehearse and revise this scene several times in sequence. With each rehearsal, they become increasingly serious as they interrogate and interpret the text more deeply. Already in the second rehearsal (Figure 3.7), the students' bodies shift and their embodied commitment to the performance takes shape. Oscar stands straight up, without recourse to his lines; he looks straight ahead as Nellie places his hands behind his back and he utters, "And I did not speak out, because I was not a Socialist." Dana now looks down contemplatively as she waits her turn to perform. Kristin's gaze is directed forward toward an audience and slightly down as if she anticipates her body's fate.

In their third rehearsal, the students now embody each element of the quotation stone-faced and Nellie falls back without anyone being there to break her fall. From the first rehearsal (Figure 3.6) to the third rehearsal (Figure 3.8) you can see bodies mediating students' thinking. It's almost as if Niemöller's central point is gradually unveiled with each rehearsal, and students' bodies reflect the gravity of his message. Enriquez's (2016) concept of body-poems is

FIGURE 3.6 Oscar, Dana, and Kristin smile, laugh, and smirk during the first rehearsal of their dramatic performance of Niemöller's text

Video Still: James S. Chisholm.

FIGURE 3.7 Nellie, Oscar, Dana, and Kristin rehearse their dramatic performance for a second time, with increasing seriousness
Video Still: James S. Chisholm.

FIGURE 3.8 Oscar, Nellie, Dana, and Kristin rehearse their dramatic performance of Niemöller's text for a third time
Video Still: James S. Chisholm.

helpful here, to see the changes students make with their bodies as increasingly affective transactions. Students' body-poems reflect their critical transaction and transformed interpretations of the text they are becoming. Visible in their body-poems are students' shifts in transacting with the text. In their first rehearsal, students take an efferent stance and seek out information in Niemöller's text for use in their performance. Students embody a more aesthetic stance as they think and feel and become the text.

FIGURE 3.9 Dana, Nellie, and Kristin perform their staged performance of Niemöller's text
Video Still: James S. Chisholm.

The students are rehearsing for a Staged Performance in front of the entire eighth grade and invited community guests, including Fred Gross, a local Holocaust survivor who has shared his story with the class. (Mr. Gross also traveled with Fred Whittaker's class, as described in Chapter 2. We share more of his story in Chapter 4.) In their last rehearsal before the performance, the group revises Nellie's final move one more time. Instead of falling down when there was "no one left to speak for me," Nellie drops to her knees, raises her hands in the air, and stares directly out at the audience, seeming to invite viewers to consider how they, too, are implicated in the responsibility to remember (USHMM, The interior; Yolen, 1988). Later, when we ask Nellie to think about this process with the VLA, she notes that they made this change "because we wanted more of [a] helpless effect. That I didn't have anyone [to speak for me]." Figure 3.9 shows Nellie's, Dana's, and Kristin's body positions in the final performance on stage.

As students embody meanings in the Niemöller text, they transform their interpretations and stances toward the content. Each time they reread, they feel the text in deeper, more serious, and more abstract ways. We recognize how these revisions are comparable to revision in the writing process. Each iteration of the students' movements layers their embodied messages and increases the likelihood that their meanings will be communicated to an audience. Also in parallel to written composition, the presence of an authentic audience elevates the students' desire to make meaning and be heard. In this case, the students' performance extends an invitation to their audience to consider their own consciences and responsibilities as they fail and succeed in speaking out against the oppression of others.

"Oh, Ring, Ring, Open Wide and Let Us Out!"

For their final Staged Performance, Tiffany's students also embody and voice *The Diary* through dramatic readings of some of Anne's most haunting and powerful diary passages.

For example, Kristin and her eighth-grade classmates select to dramatize the following November 8, 1943, entry:

> I see the eight of us in the Annex as if we were a patch of blue sky surrounded by menacing black clouds. The perfectly round spot on which we're standing is still safe, but the clouds are moving in on us, and the ring between us and the approaching danger is being pulled tighter and tighter. We're surrounded by darkness and danger, and in our desperate search for a way out we keep bumping into each other. We look at the fighting down below and the peace and beauty up above. In the meantime, we've been cut off by the dark mass of clouds, so that we can go neither up nor down. It looms before us like an impenetrable wall, trying to crush us, but not yet able to. I can only cry out and implore, "Oh, ring, ring, open wide and let us out!"
>
> (Frank, 1952, p. 143)

The students consider ways of representing at once the many persons in the close quarters of the annex and the "dark clouds" as they impose on everyone's consciousness. Kristin kneels on the ground, encircled by six of her classmates and rehearses the lines: "We're surrounded by darkness and danger." As she speaks the next words, her classmates take steps toward her, using their bodies to feel and become the cramped spaces within which Anne and seven others moved about in the annex: "And in our desperate search for a way out we keep bumping into each other."

In their deliberations about the ways to represent the content of the passage, students identify the lines "so that we can go neither up nor down" as an image to seize and they rehearse raising their arms up on the word "up" and slowly bringing their hands and fingers down on the word "down" (Figure 3.10). At that point, Kristin exclaims the final words from this entry: "Oh, ring, ring, open wide and let us out!" Upon uttering these concluding words in a sharp, loud voice, Kristin's classmates shoot their arms up into the air and turn away from her scream, as if they are actually *opening* to let Anne and the others out of the annex and away from the horrific circumstances that surround them.

After running through their first attempt to enact the passage, the students recognize the power in their performances and smile about the way it felt to convey the meaning in words through movement in their bodies. After turning away from Kristin, they quickly snap back toward her and immediately begin thinking about revision. Their excited talk indicates their collective desire to create something specific and meaningful with their bodies and gestures. As they brainstorm ideas, Oscar asks specifically about the shape his fingers should be in as they encroach upon Kristin ("Anne"). The fingers should be "menacing," the group members decide and then clench their hands into claw shapes during the subsequent performance (see Figures 3.11 and 3.12).

Being a spectator is a powerful element of performance in arts-based inquiry. As Edmiston (2011) notes,

> The performance dimension of dramatic inquiry means that as young people watch and listen to fictional presentations by peers, adults, or via electronic media, they may reflect for the possible meanings of what is being or has been, represented. Without shifting to take up a spectator stance they cannot analyze events critically.
>
> (p. 227)

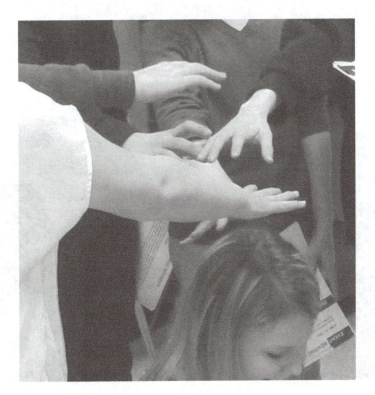

FIGURE 3.10 Kristin's group represents "We've been cut off by the dark mass of clouds, so that we can go neither up nor down"
Video Still: James S. Chisholm.

FIGURE 3.11 Students contort their fingers into menacing shapes
Video Still: James S. Chisholm.

FIGURE 3.12 Oscar practices moving his menacing fingers toward Kristin
Video Still: James S. Chisholm.

The VLA process promotes such reflection and analysis explicitly by inviting students who perform texts and those who view them to write and talk about nonlinguistic modes of representation and the meanings such representations convey.

Kristin selects a photograph of this engagement for a VLA, shared in Figure 3.13. She wraps her response to the prompts around the photo. Her reflection begins with a number of descriptive sentences above the image: "I am looking toward 'the audience,'" "Their hands are reaching out to grab me," "I am kneeling on the ground." As her writing continues, her sentences become more analytical: "it makes me look weak," and "There isn't much empathy in my picture because as I'm playing Anne, I know that no one was really there to help her."

During the VLA discussion, Kathy asks Kristin what it felt like to rehearse this scene. Kristin says, "It was really interesting to try to be," as she air quotes with her fingers, "in Anne's shoes because I did learn a lot from her diary." She continues, "It made me, it put into perspective, like how bad her and her family had to suffer."

Another student in the VLA discussion, Shannon, chimes in, "I think when we're rehearsing it, we don't put as much performing into it, as much as we could. But once we're on stage, we take the persona of the person we're trying to become." Kristin's and Shannon's responses are evidence of their learning about Anne Frank and drama techniques, reflected during the VLA, which documents moments of embodied literacies learning.

Empathy!

In this picture I am looking towards "the audience". The rest of the group is looking down on to ~~me~~. Their hands are reaching out to grab me as I

perform / my monoloug
I am / kneeling on
the ground / while the
group / is leaning
toward me. / As I am
on the gr... / it makes
me look / weak
We all / are very
close / together,
which / makes it
look like / I'm being
closed / in on.

I believe I was taking a risk really getting into my monolouge, in a sort of way I was very emotional performing as Anne and that took a lot of courage. People are quickly moving towards me. there isn't much empathy in my picture because as I'm playing Anne, I know that no one was really there to help her.

FIGURE 3.13 Kristin's Visual Learning Analysis (VLA) text unpacks a moment of embodied literacies learning

Photo: James S. Chisholm.

LAYERING EMBODIED LITERACIES

Evident across the examples we draw on in this chapter are students moving and freezing movement to learn about Anne Frank and the Holocaust *through* and *in* their bodies. In other words, students use their bodies to mediate their learning about Anne Frank's diary and the historical context within which the Holocaust took place. But students also learn *in* their bodies as they intuit movement from a visual icon during a dramatic reading and read gestures and gazes to respond to classmates in Tableau. Students learn *in* their bodies when they sense the desire of a sculptor to mold intelligent clay in particular ways in Sculpture Garden. And students learn *in* their bodies when their facial, postural, and gestural expressions shift as they perceive the gravity of language of a Holocaust text. Finally, students learn *in* their bodies when they experiment with contorting their fingers to create the precise effect of "menacing" in Dramatic and Staged Performances.

Embodying texts leads to layered understandings of *The Diary* through multiple and multi-semiotic readings of the text. Students use their bodies to mediate thinking about challenging texts and situate the locus of knowledge *in* the body rather than solely in the mind or the text (Claxton, 2015; Micciche, 2007). Key to embodying texts, and not unlike other literacies learning, revising performative responses to texts promotes new analytical perspectives for those creating the embodied composition and for those deconstructing it critically—the audience of learners and spectators in this case. Being the text affords classrooms the space within which challenging texts can be studied deeply. In short, embodying texts creates the conditions necessary for students to empathize with Anne Frank's diary, and make contemporary connections, a topic toward which we turn in the next chapter.

REFERENCES

Albers, P. (2006). Imagining the possibilities in multimodal curriculum design. *English Education, 38*(2), 75–101.

Chisholm, J. S., & Whitmore, K. F. (2016). Bodies in space/bodies in motion/bodies in character: Adolescents bear witness to Anne Frank. *International Journal of Education and the Arts, 17*(5). Retrieved from www.ijea.org/v/17n5/

Claxton, G. (2015). *Intelligence in the flesh: Why your mind needs your body much more than it thinks.* New Haven, CT: Yale University Press.

Edmiston, B. (2011). Teaching for transformation: Drama and language arts education. In D. Lapp & D. Fisher (Eds.), *The handbook of research on teaching the English language arts* (pp. 224–230). New York, NY: Erlbaum.

Edmiston, B. (2014). *Transforming teaching and learning with active and dramatic approaches: Engaging students across the curriculum.* New York, NY: Routledge.

Enriquez, G. (2016). Reader response and embodied performance: Body-poems as performative response and performativity. In G. Enriquez, E. Johnson, S. Kontovourki, & C. A. Mallozzi (Eds.), *Literacies, learning, and the body: Putting theory and research into pedagogical practice* (pp. 41–56). New York, NY: Routledge.

Frank, A. (1952). *The diary of a young girl.* New York, NY: Bantam.

Lakoff, G., & Johnson, M. (1999). *Philosophy in the flesh: The embodied mind and its challenge to western thought.* New York, NY: Basic Books.

Landay, E., & Wootton, K. (2012). *A reason to read: Linking literacy and the arts.* Cambridge, MA: Harvard Education Press.

Leavy, P. (2015). *Method meets art: Arts-based research practice* (2nd ed.). New York, NY: The Guilford Press.

Micciche, L. (2007). *Doing emotion.* Portsmouth, NH: Boynton/Cook Publishers.

Rosenblatt, L. (1978). *The reader, the text, the poem: The transactional theory of the literary work.* Carbondale: Southern Illinois University Press.

Rubin, J. E. (2000). *Teaching about the Holocaust through drama.* Charlottesville, VA: New Plays.

Schmidt, R. (2009). Finding our way with teachers and families: Reading and responding to the Holocaust. In K. M. Leander, D. W. Rowe, D. K. Dickinson, M. K. Hundley, R. T. Jiménez, & V. J. Risko (Eds.), *58th yearbook of the national reading conference* (pp. 248–260). Oak Creek, WI: National Reading Conference.

Siegel, M. (1995). More than words: The generative power of transmediation for learning. *Canadian Journal of Education, 20*(4), 455–475.

Sipe, L. R. (2002). Talking back and taking over: Young children's expressive engagement during storybook read-alouds. *The Reading Teacher, 55*(5), 476–483.

Snowber, C. (2012). Dancing a curriculum of hope: Cultivating passion as an embodied inquiry. *Journal of Curriculum Theorizing, 28*(2), 118–125.

Towndrow, P. A., Nelson, M. E., & Yusuf, W. F. B. M. (2013). Squaring literacy assessment with multi-modal design: An analytic case for semiotic awareness. *Journal of Literacy Research, 45*(4), 327–355.

USHMM. (n.d.). The Interior: The Hall of Remembrance. Retrieved from: www.ushmm.org/information/about-the-museum/architecture-and-art/inside-the-museum-the-hall-of-remembrance

Whitmore, K. F. (2015). "Becoming the story" in the joyful world of Jack and the Beanstalk. *Language Arts, 93*(1), 25–37.

Wilson, G. P. (2003). Supporting young children's thinking through tableau. *Language Arts, 80*(5), 375–383.

Woodcock, C. (2010). "I allow myself to FEEL now…": Adolescent girls' negotiations of embodied knowing, the female body, and literacy. *Journal of Literacy Research, 42*(4), 349–384.

Yolen, J. (1988). *The devil's arithmetic*. New York, NY: Puffin.

Chapter 4
Feeling the Text

During a Visual Learning Analysis (VLA) in Kelly Holland's eighth-grade English Language Arts class, Lucy chooses an image of students taken as they examine the cordel early in their study. The students in the photo are visibly close to one another, looking intently at a set of photographs taken by Mendel Grossman while he was imprisoned for being a Jew in the Łódź Ghetto during World War II. (A collection of Grossman's photography is compiled in *My Secret Camera: Life in the Łódź Ghetto*, Smith & Grossman, 2008.) After describing literally what was happening when the VLA photo was taken, Lucy continues to write on the VLA in Figure 4.1:

> I felt bad, really, honestly horrible when I learned about it. Truthfully, I don't think I can sympathize well, but when I saw something this gruesome, I couldn't help but think "Why?" A few nights while we were studying the Holocaust while I was thinking of and doing diary entries I would always ask myself "Why?" Why didn't anyone help? Why did this happen? If I were there could I have changed anything?

The VLA creates a space for this student to reflect and ask the question that demonstrates deep learning and has haunted all of those who lived through and after the Holocaust: Why?

In this chapter, we characterize the learning that is expressed during responses like Lucy's as *feeling the text*. We conceptualize emotion as a layer that deepens literacies learning and validates and exposes the complexities of challenging texts. *Feeling the text* allows students to get closer to the experiences and emotions of characters and inhabit, even temporarily and vicariously, their experiences. Emotions do not emerge as a mere by-product of reading or learning (e.g. tearing up at the end of a sad story); rather, like bodies (see Chapter 3), emotions mediate literacies learning.

Although emotions have traditionally been perceived to be objects of control in schools (Lewis & Tierney, 2013), we explore in this chapter the ways in which emotions can be used to circulate stories into and out of classrooms and broader communities. We conceptualize this process of bringing stories in from the community and moving stories out into the community as *mobilizing* emotion. Mobilizing emotion into communities can promote agency for students

At this point, I'm pretty sure this a picture was close to the beginning of our unit, at the point where we were just beginning to learn about the Holocaust. I sure most of us were looking at the photos, on the pieces of paper, but there were still some people not really focusing.

Okay, so my thoughts for this are that the photos really did help. It formed an image and a story for me. It was a broad story, but it gave me an idea on what the Holocaust was and is. I felt bad, really, honestly horrible when I learned about it. Truthfully, I don't think I can sympathize well, but when I saw something this gruesome, I couldn't help but think "Why?" A few nights while we were studying the Holocaust while I was thinking & doing diary entries I would always ask myself "Why?" Why didn't anyone help? Why did this happen? If I were there could I have changed anything?

FIGURE 4.1 Lucy's Visual Learning Analysis (VLA) emphasizes enduring emotional questions about the Holocaust

and teachers. *Feeling the text* allows adolescent readers of challenging texts to become powerful agents in their own literacies learning and to recognize how their emotional responses are deepening their understandings of challenging texts and contexts. As Boler (1999) notes, *"Feeling power … refers to the power of feeling*—a power largely untapped in Western cultures in which we learn to fear and control emotions" (p. 4).

The emotion of empathy is a targeted goal for some teachers. Empathizing is certainly a literacy practice that could transform a world in which so many people are disregarded, rendered invisible, actively marginalized, exploited, and killed because of their otherness—a central lesson of the Holocaust that seems to have been forgotten, or perhaps never learned, in contemporary society. Yet, empathy is potentially a problematic response for the study of *The Diary* as it may easily result in students romanticizing Anne's experiences or diluting the Holocaust into trite statements or meaningless clichés (Gray, 2015). Clearly, it is impossible for students (or adults) to feel Anne's feelings as a German-born Jew living in Amsterdam during the first half of the 20th century; or in the annex in hiding with seven other people, some of them strangers to her; or in the Bergen-Belsen camp where Anne ultimately died of typhus. Thus "empathy" like any concept (Vygotsky, 1986) cannot be taught or learned in a vacuum; rather, empathy, we argue, is mediated through visual and embodied literacies, which further mediates emotional understandings of Anne's narrative. Such layered experiences provide students with multiple perspectives from which to view Anne's story and her surrounding circumstances.

The power of images and the disturbing factual content of the Holocaust provoke intensely emotional responses among students and teachers studying this history. Eighth graders are often earnestly expressive about their emotions. Sometimes they say and write statements directed to Anne. Lillian shares, "And if there can be hope when there is darkness surrounding you, then hope can survive anywhere. Because of you, we know that hope is indestructible." And Valerie writes,

You have impacted this world so much and you don't even know. Today people accept each other for who they are and many have kinder hearts. You have not only educated many but have changed many hearts such as mine. You have helped me to show more empathy and to be more open minded about people and their beliefs.

The students' messages, naive or simplistic as they may be, are representative of their emotions as they read, think, dramatize, create, and learn. Furthermore, the capacity to try on the perspective of another person is integral to many fundamental literacy practices including literature discussion groups, transactional reading experiences, and writing for an authentic audience. Literacy researchers conceptualize such relational literacy practices as 21st-century literacy skills (Beach, Thein, & Webb, 2012). As Louise Rosenblatt says, "Literature ... helps readers develop the imaginative capacity to put themselves in the place of others—a capacity essential in a democracy, where we need to rise above narrow self-interest and envision the broader human consequences of political decisions" (Karolides & Rosenblatt, 1999, p. 169).

Emotion plays a mediating role in classrooms where students are reading challenging texts; there are affordances and challenges of feeling texts in classrooms. Micciche (2007) says "we do emotions—they don't simply happen to us" (p. 2). She continues, "Emotion is experienced between people within a particular context (and so resides both *in* people and *in* culture) and that emotion is an expression, experience, and perception mediated by language, body, and culture" (pp. 7–8, emphasis in original). Emotionally mediated literacy experiences allow one to imagine the context of another, thereby providing multiple perspectives on texts and the capacity to draw on those perspectives to act in the world—*feeling power*, to use Boler's (1999) terminology.

As we describe in Chapters 2 and 3, schools privilege the linguistic sign system over the visual sign system and disembodied learning over movement. Similarly, students' minds (e.g. achievement, answering questions correctly, being "on task") are treated as separate and more valued entities over their emotions. So, too, are some emotions (e.g. happiness) permitted in school while others are deemed inappropriate (e.g. anger). We find it impossible, however, to decouple feeling and thinking. As Claxton (2015) argues, "Feelings ... are the bodily glue that sticks our reasoning and our common sense together. Feelings are somatic events that embody our values and concerns" (p. 5). Just as with *seeing the text* (visual reading) and *being the text* (embodied reading), *feeling the text* (emotional reading) is co-constructed between learners and mediated by activity that goes beyond words.

Drawing on all of these ideas about emotion in literacies learning classrooms, in this chapter we illustrate how *feeling the text* compels students and teachers to experience Anne Frank's diary in nontrivial ways, which leads learners to consider their affective and relational stances toward the consequences of the Holocaust in the past, the present, and in the future.

MAKING MEANING THROUGH EMOTION

In the first section of this chapter, firsthand interactions with Holocaust survivors contextualize the genocide historically by Creating Thick Air—an affective intensity described below that is conducive to working with challenging texts and brings emotion from the community into the classroom. Next, engaging multimodally through music, dance, and spoken word, Contemporary Connections further mobilizes students' emotions to connect the circumstances surrounding the Holocaust to their real, current lives, and to the social and cultural circumstances that encircle them. Finally, students use Marquee to move emotion from their classroom into their community, which creates a call to action when an act of vandalism leads students to respond to the incident.

Feeling the Past: Creating Thick Air

Precisely because it won't always be possible to hear eyewitness accounts from Holocaust survivors, we document here the effect of inviting survivors and their family members to share their stories with students. These encounters infuse emotion into classroom environments, thereby sanctioning *feeling the text* as students read *The Diary* and other challenging texts. We call this process Creating Thick Air. We can't create deep and meaningful moments "out of thin air." Creating Thick Air inspires creativity and risk-taking in a safe learning space, which Landay and Wootton (2012) argue is a precondition for deep and meaningful learning experiences. In Chapter 5, Eileen Landay elaborates on additional practices that support Creating Thick Air as part of classroom community building.

"A Beautiful Piece of Life"

In his memoir, *One Step Ahead of Hitler: A Jewish Child's Journey Through France*, journalist Fred Gross (2010) tells his Holocaust story. It documents his time as a small child when, with his family, he escaped the Nazi invasion of Belgium and France and was smuggled into Switzerland before immigrating to the United States. Because he was only three years old when he and his family members began their journey through France, Mr. Gross relied on his brothers' and mother's accounts to supplement his memory of that emotionally charged period in his life. His book is the result of piecing together moments recalled by Mr. Gross and fleshed out in research and interviews with family members. Mr. Gross now speaks widely to students across the country. He speaks at many of the schools featured in this book, sometimes accompanies Fred Whittaker's students on their trips to the United States Holocaust Memorial Museum (USHMM), and is actively involved in community activities throughout Louisville.

Teacher Voice Box

The art and architecture of the Holocaust Memorial are meant to go beyond merely creating a container for artifacts. There is a whispered narrative: the place, the lights, everything about the Memorial whispers emotively to you, informing and creating a soulful context for visitors' journey through it.

Fred Whittaker, science and religion teacher

During his visit to Tiffany LaVoie's eighth-grade drama class, Mr. Gross shares a slideshow he's prepared for students. The slides include pictures from his family photo album and maps of the places in Europe where his family hid, were interned, and lived openly. His story features suspense, fortune, and trauma, which quickly capture students' attention, respect, and admiration. After revealing to students the remarkable circumstances in which he happened across a photograph online of him and his family on a truck as he conducted research for his memoir, he closes his presentation with an iconic image of shoes from Holocaust victims that are part of the permanent exhibit of the USHMM, above which is reproduced an excerpt from Moishe Schulstein's poem "I Saw a Mountain."

Mr. Gross tells the class,

These are shoes. They're in the Holocaust museum; they were preserved by the Nazis as evidence of what they were doing to the Jewish people. This is just the example of one, and up here it reads. 'Shoes. Little shoes, big shoes. We are the shoes, we are the last witnesses. /We are shoes from grandchildren and grandfathers, /From Prague, Paris and Amsterdam, /And because we are only made of fabric and leather /And not of blood and flesh, each one of us avoided the hellfire.' That was written by a Jewish poet. I have shoes, too. These are my baby shoes … do you want to see the real thing?

Mr. Gross reaches into his coat pocket and pulls out a pair of very small shoes, made of soft white leather. "These are my baby shoes that my mother held onto during our journey. You want to touch them?"

Mr. Gross wraps up his talk and says, "Well, this is the end of my story children," and the class applauds. Holding his baby shoes, Mr. Gross reflects out loud,

Imagine my mother holding on to this beautiful piece of life. Can you imagine what this meant to her? I didn't know she had them until after she died in 1989, and I went through her belongings and I found these shoes.

As he's gathering his belongings to leave, Mr. Gross remarks,

One other thing, when I came to this country [in 1946 as a 10-year-old boy], came on a boat, and we docked in Norfolk, Virginia. [We] went to the train station to wait for the train to take us to New York, I went to the bathroom … and I saw an elderly man, skin darker than I had ever seen before. We walked out together, didn't say anything, he gave me a smile. I walk out and I see two young White boys talking to my brother, Leo, who was sitting on a bench. I had a feeling something was going on, so I ask my brother—listen carefully, 1946; it was the South—I ask my brother, Leo, 'What's happening?' and my brother told me that I walked into the wrong restroom.

Mr. Gross looks directly at a student in the front row. "Can you tell me what kind of restroom I walked into?" Michelle answers, "One for African Americans."
Mr. Gross continues,

Uh-hum. How 'bout that? My first day on American soil, and I witness discrimination against a certain group of people. It made a tremendous impact on me, especially when I was a reporter later on in New Haven, Connecticut, and I reported on the Civil Rights Movement, and on discrimination and persecution of African Americans. I did a number of stories on them. It was 1966, I remember, I wrote some stories, 45 years later I get a letter from one of the young Black activists that I knew, thanking me for what I did. For giving them voice through my reporting.
Tiffany asks, "Mr. Gross, do you have any parting words for us?"

And Mr. Gross answers,

Parting words? Well, yes. I wouldn't be here today without the courage of people who helped us out. It took a lot of guts, they risked their lives to save a Jewish family, and there may come a point in your life where you may have to stand up and be counted. A good friend of mine said, talking about bystanders, from a moral point of view; there may be no such thing as a bystander. If you are there, watching people being bullied, watching injustices being brought on people, if you're just standing there, you are taking part. You are just as guilty as the perpetrators. Remember that. Good lesson to learn.

I'm learning, I don't know everything. I don't expect you, for example, to see a kid being beaten up by twenty people and then coming in and trying to rescue them. But, call somebody, call your teacher. Let 'em know what's going on.

Mr. Gross's story affects students deeply. And his shoes are semiotic artifacts (Figure 4.2). "Objects can be described as 'semiotic' when they are bound up with an act of meaning making" (Pahl & Rowsell, 2010, p. 39). In reflections that Tiffany's students write, they demonstrate the power of Mr. Gross's story. Kristin says, "When I saw Mr. Gross' baby shoes I was astonished because first of all, it was amazing how his mother kept those shoes all throughout the year[s] and also it showed how young he was during the war." And Natalie notes,

His description of the German aircrafts dropping down not only shocked me, but now that I reflect, it brought me close to tears. He was just a child and … seeing even strangers around you die could make you scared. That is why he could've thought that the next time it would be him and/or his family.

These reflections point to the semiotic power of the artifacts in Mr. Gross's story.

Student Voice Box

I will stand up for people and not be a bystander.

Dana, eighth-grade student

Teacher Voice Box

The students were most impressive, in my opinion, by the way in which they took the content seriously… Everybody put this idea of empathy [first] and how important it is to have empathy, to see how much your empathy is needed in the world, and to take action—and that your action can and will have an impact that is meaningful.

Tiffany LaVoie, drama teacher

Mr. Gross's Holocaust story and his baby shoes are part of Creating Thick Air. His shoes support emotional responses to his story. They "smell; they can be felt, heard, listened to, and looked at" (Pahl & Rowsell, 2010, p. 10). The students can *feel* Mr. Gross's story as they think about their own childhood artifacts, familial love, and the fragility of life.

Mr. Gross's concluding remarks about his arrival in the United States also bring into focus the critical relevance of his Holocaust story in the time and place of the students in Tiffany's classroom. In a reflection on Mr. Gross's visit, Kristin writes:

Three things that stood out to me were Mr. Gross' baby shoes and how his mother kept them, how the Gross family escaped Gurs [internment camp in France], and how quickly the family went from dressing nicely to dressing in rags.

Similarly, Tasha identifies the shoes and bathroom scenes as most meaningful and provides her reasoning why: "These things stood out to me because I could imagine the hurt and pain he went

FIGURE 4.2 Mr. Gross hands to a drama student the baby shoes his mother kept with her as their family escaped Nazi persecution
Photo: Jeffrey Jamner.

through." Pahl and Rowsell (2010) emphasize how artifacts tell their own stories, connect meanings across space and time, and make it possible for "domain crossing" (p. 16) to occur between school and out-of-school settings.

Teacher Voice Box

Some of my students who ... struggle to engage—no matter what we're doing—were fully engaged after they saw that this was real. And that this changed the lives and ended the lives of so many people. And that they were entrusted with telling this story and sharing how important it is to get involved and to speak up so that atrocities like this eventually can be stopped.

Tiffany LaVoie, drama teacher

"They Were Afraid"

Michael Schubert, the son of Holocaust survivors, shares his family's Holocaust survival story with many students as they read *The Diary*. Michael's parents survived the Holocaust as teenagers before immigrating to the United States. His story is about his mother, who convinces a Nazi soldier to let her and her mother escape a line that would have certainly led to their murders.

Kelly Holland's students are fortunate to learn from Michael's story, which they hear before they read *The Diary* and serves to activate the emotional context of their study of the Holocaust. They are seated in a semi-circle around Michael on the stage in the school auditorium. Michael begins,

> So my mom was always kind of a gutsy person. And she didn't know what had gotten into her that day. But as she was walking past the guard to her death, she burst out laughing, hysterical laughing. And the guard turned to her and said, 'You. Why are you laughing? Don't you know what's about to happen to you?' And she said, 'Yeah, I know what's going to happen to me. I'm laughing because, what could a child possibly have done to deserve this? Why are you killing children? What crime could we have done in our short lives to deserve this?'

As his story continues, students lean in and keep their eyes in contact with Michael's:

> 'I'm going to haunt you. That's why I'm laughing. You are never going to sleep again. I'm going to haunt you for the rest of your life' my mom warned. The soldier was kind of amused by her and he said, 'Big mouth! Scram!' And my grandmother, who was standing next to her, probably around 30 or so at the time, whispered to my mother, 'Does he mean me too?' And my mother, at that moment, was the adult of the two of them. She said 'Shut up and come.' And that's why I'm sitting here talking to you today.

After the story, Samuel asks Michael, "Does the Holocaust still haunt you?" To answer, Michael knocks loudly on the wooden floor of the stage—BANG, BANG, BANG. He says about his parents, "They were afraid" and describes how sometimes they reacted with fear, for example, at a loud knock on their apartment door, which might have reminded them of the pounding of a rifle butt of someone who was coming for them.

After a moment of quiet, Jane Dewey, a guest teaching artist who is providing Kelly with support for trying new arts-based strategies, asks the students to approach an instructional activity she has prepared "with the same thoughtfulness that you approached Michael's story," and to think about the following line in particular: "They were afraid." She asks them to write a fear they have on a half-sheet of paper,

> And I'd like you—if you can, in this moment—to use your response to the story to take you to a thoughtful place where it goes a little bit beyond 'I'm afraid of spiders.' … think a little bit deeper about a fear that has a little more tension for you… Don't put your names on these … just fold them in half and give them to me. Do this solo so you're not looking at anyone else's. No one is going to know whose it is … so these are completely yours. We're going to use them, but not in a way that anyone will know that it's yours.

Students write silently for about two and a half minutes, many of them stretched out on their stomachs on the floor, and then hand their papers and markers to Kelly or Jane (Figure 4.3).

As Michael shares his story and his parents' testimony, he's creating thick air in which students are more likely to risk telling their own stories and articulating their own fears. Jane invites students to build on Michael's story by naming their fears before meaningfully representing those fears using their bodies to "freeze" the ideas that haunt them. As our ArtsLiteracy

FIGURE 4.3 Students think and write about something that scares them
Photo: Kathryn F. Whitmore.

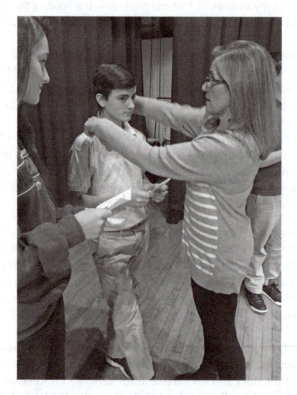

FIGURE 4.4 Kelly Holland helps two students brainstorm options for creating a frozen
shape for a fear
Photo: Kathryn F. Whitmore.

- Everyone was closely paying attention.

- I think this was the most interesting thing we did during this project.

- Everyone looked serious about what the speaker was talking about.

- Everyone was relaxed

- Everyone seemed like they were only interested in the speaker.

- Their faces were stern, but not like they were mad. It seemed more like they were sad or maybe pondering about what the speaker was saying.

- Majority of us had our hands in our laps not playing with anything. No one was distracted.

- Our teacher looked as if she was concerned

FIGURE 4.5 Dasia's Visual Learning Analysis (VLA) emphasizes the emotional effect of Michael's story

colleague, Len Newman, says, regarding Creating Thick Air, "If you tell them a good story, you're going to get a good story back." Next, Jane pairs students and asks them to create three frozen shapes (see Chapter 2 for further description of Tableau) to capture what haunts them. In Figure 4.4, Kelly supports students' embodied meaning making.

To complete a VLA, Dasia selects a photograph that depicts Michael sitting on the stage with her class. Her responses to our prompts and questions are rich with references to emotion. When we ask her to think about the facial expressions and locations of hands in the photograph, for example, Dasia notices that the "Majority of us had our hands in our laps not playing with anything" and that "No one was distracted" (see Figure 4.5). She notes that "Everyone was relaxed" and "looked serious." "Their faces were stern," she continues, "but not like they were mad. It seemed more like they were sad or maybe pondering."

The photograph allows Dasia to return to the moment of emotional learning. Dasia's comments on the attentiveness the students give to Michael teach us that his story is creating thick air, and that it resonates for her. She marks this event as "the most interesting thing we did during this project."

Feeling the Present: Contemporary Connections

At Kim Joiner's school, it's the final performance of the class's study of *The Diary*. As parents, other eighth graders, and community members fill the theater space, projections of text and images on either side of the stage call attention to the title of the performance: "What is Your Humanity Footprint?" A solitary desk is visible, stage left, and nothing else. On the column behind the desk are juxtaposed images of the students and historical persons they are portraying (Figure 4.6).

Collectively, the students create, write, and design a Staged Performance called "What is Your Humanity Footprint?" It includes linguistic texts—excerpts from *The Diary*, historical primary source documents, poetry, and student-written monologues—that connect Anne Frank's story with contemporary social justice issues. Coupled with music, dance, and visual arts texts,

FIGURE 4.6 The visual "playbill" showing roles students play in their final staged performance
Photo: James S. Chisholm.

the students author a new multimodal text to reflect Anne's context, voice, and emotion. The performance begins with a reading from the beginning of *The Diary*.

To provide historical context and perspective on the circumstances in which Anne wrote her diary, one type of performance is dramatic scene acting in which radio broadcasts chronicle military advancements during the war (see Figure 4.7). This particular aspect of the performance means students have reason to research newspaper headlines and articles from World War II. They learn about the format of such radio broadcasts, including the music that marked the news, the static that would have been audible, and the look of radios. These scenes provide an historical timeline of the major events of World War II and contextualize the passages from Anne's diary that a group of students pantomime. The radio scenes provide a structure that promotes narrative coherence, and gives students with interests in history, technology, and design opportunities to co-author the performance and become visible in their own way.

Emotion acts in these scenes to mediate students' layered literacy experiences. Radio broadcasters inflect their voices to express the emotions that undergird their proclamations. Radio

FIGURE 4.7 Students, in character in the annex, gather around the radio to listen to broadcasts about the war
Photo: James S. Chisholm.

listeners use their bodies to show the emotions they are "feeling" as they lean in toward the radio, bite their fingernails, and furrow their brows in response to the content of the broadcast.

Interspersed with the scenes from *The Diary* are ensemble performances about contemporary topics in response to the emotional nature of the historical context. For example, Amy writes and performs a monologue about rape culture that includes this section:

> When girls are afraid to walk down the street alone or at night, that is rape culture. When they will only feel safe if they have pepper spray and keys between their fingers as weapons, that is rape culture. When people laugh at jokes about rape and sexual assault, that is rape culture. When male artists release songs about a so-called grey area of consent and receive little backlash, that is rape culture. When young girls are told that they can't show a *shoulder*, that is rape culture.

Amy's monologue mobilizes emotion as it connects the audience to her story. The rhetorical use of repetition in her performance further circulates emotion between each member of the audience and herself. Amy's intonations, posture, and authority in performance call to mind Micciche's (2007) claim that emotion that is "produced *between* people" in performance creates "more complexity and dimension … than does a purely textual orientation" (pp. 7–8).

Some students become visible and author their own stories across artistic mediums to connect their reading of Anne's diary with contemporary and often immediate circumstances. Callie choreographs an interpretive dance that raises awareness about destructive discourses that circulate in schools around body image, especially for young women. Danielle recites a letter written by a classmate who talks back against the bullies and bullying that led her to suicidal ideation. Finally, Monique performs Ernestine Johnson's spoken word poem, "The Average Black Girl," which articulates a series of oppressive perceptions and actions endured and overcome by African American girls and women, as well as the extraordinary accomplishments of African American women civil rights leaders like Ella Baker and Diane Nash. Johnson's poem concludes, "I am not the average black girl, I can only aspire to be."

Making contemporary connections through multiple art forms captivates the audience. As Eisner (2002) says, "The arts provide a spectrum of such forms—we call them visual arts, music, dance, theater—through which meanings are made, revised, shared, and discovered. These forms enable us to construct meanings that are nonredundant" (p. 230). Such contemporary connections with Anne Frank's narrative are made even more poignant as they are woven throughout a multimodal ensemble that includes dramatic embodied performances from Anne's diary, interview video with a local Holocaust survivor, and expository and visual texts that document emotional readings of the Holocaust.

Student Voice Box

Finding a woman that was 5 years old, living in Germany during the Holocaust—that is so rare. So being able to meet someone and talk to them … and interview them… Keeping the story going is so important because everybody that was there is … leaving, and not going to be here for too much longer, so bringing that historical context to the table is so important because if us, as kids, don't know about it, then the story would just die. We have to keep it going.

Amy, eighth-grade student

Feeling the Future: Marquee

Fred Whittaker and his students use their school's marquee to reproduce passages from *The Diary* as a call for the community's collective reflection on Anne Frank's words and life (see Figure 4.8).

Not unlike its use at other institutions, the marquee is typically used by the school as a public bulletin board of sorts and includes reminders about important upcoming dates and congratulatory messages for different student group or team accomplishments. During their study of

Anne Frank and the Holocaust, and well beyond its conclusion, Fred and his students use Marquee to highlight diary passages that passersby can consider as a reflection of contemporary or future society. Some of the passages that Fred and his students select are:

> Anne Marie Frank
> 1929–1945
> "I am still alive but don't ask me why or how."
> Anne Marie Frank
> 1929–1945
> "The entrance to our hiding place has been properly concealed."
> Anne Marie Frank
> 1929–1945
> "I still believe, in spite of everything, that people are truly good at heart."

It's impossible to know what passersby think or feel when they read Anne Frank's words on the school's marquee. Yet we do know that the messages provoke students' reflection and function to connect the content of one class's curriculum with the broader community in which that class is situated. We see this novel use of the marquee as a way to engage the entire community in the conversations that students care about. Rather than containing emotion in their classroom, Marquee, like Staged Performance, mobilizes students' emotional literacies into the community.

FIGURE 4.8 The marquee outside Fred Whittaker's school. "Dearest Kitty...."
Photo: James S. Chisholm.

Teacher Voice Box

Not having had a lot of prior experience with having students move more into the text as we've done, using their bodies and tapping into emotions… I tried to do what I was taught… [I] followed the directions. But my experience was, it was truly delightful, it was informative, it was challenging. It kind of pushed—I got to ride the students' experience in parallel with them because I hadn't been through this. So there was a greater sense of empathy I had as a learner. We were kind of inhabiting the same space in terms of our comfort levels and our abilities and our skill levels. So it allowed me to be a lot more sensitive to what they were doing.

Fred Whittaker, science and religion teacher

One night, at the end of the first year of this project, the marquee is vandalized. The perpetrators remove letters from it in such a way that the only letters remaining are "KK." Students receive the news in class on the next Monday morning and have the opportunity to react and talk about what's happened. Jill feels personally affronted by the vandalism because she feels it is targeted directly at Anne Frank. She says,

It's kind of like they're disrespecting Anne Frank because this entire time we've been learning—she's our friend because we read her book and her diary. She was so close to us. The fact that someone would just disrespect her like that, it stings.

Students share a series of "tumbling emotions," which include grief, sadness, anger, and hurt. Fred invites students to focus their emotions in order to act in response to the vandalism. "What else can we do?" Fred asks, then groups students together by twos or threes to formulate response options. Students offer the following: (a) put up another sign, (b) pray for themselves and the perpetrators, and (c) publish their message on social media. Fred adopts all of these suggestions and challenges students to select a "beautiful response" from Anne's diary to post to the marquee and to get the message on social media to reach all the way to the Anne Frank House in Amsterdam. Students quickly grab copies of *The Diary* and identify selections they deem most fitting for the next marquee message. Fred narrows down the passages to three and invites students to stand by the selection that they think is the most powerful. The passage they select—perhaps *The Diary's* most famous—takes on a new and local meaning in light of these circumstances: "I still believe, in spite of everything, that people are truly good at heart" (Frank, 1952, p. 328).

Fred and his students talk about why anyone would commit such an act. They wonder together about the message that was intended, and delivered. "We don't know what happened or why," Fred says, but "There's a feeling we can get from it. We understand through what we *know* as much sometimes as what we *feel*. To me, it feels sad. What do you feel about it? What understanding are you gathering through the feeling?" Without reverting to speculation, Fred validates students' feelings as a source of learning, and allows them to express those feelings together.

Arianna remarks that she feels sad because the vandalism suggests to her that anti-Semitism is still present in the world, indeed in her own community, today. Jill reflects that she has never had anything like this happen to her before "firsthand," and recognizes her and her school's relative insulation from being the target of crime:

It's kind of like a reality check because, in our classroom, if it was really a hate [crime] against the Jewish faith, in general, we've never really experienced that firsthand. So having that happen to our own school is some sort of a reality check that it's out there and we should watch out for it.

Heather feels angry because the vandalism disrespects Anne's last wishes. She says,

Like Anne Frank's last wish was literally 'Don't let this happen again.' We're taking steps to make sure people don't forget and somebody's gone out of their way to stop that. It makes me feel really angry. This was a horrible thing that happened. You have to accept the fact and learn from it or it could happen again.

Their conversation turns to the most appropriate ways to respond, and John suggests that the class gather around the marquee and pray. Everyone agrees, and the group walks quietly down the stairs and outside to gather in a circle and talk before they join hands and pray together (see Figure 4.9). This event of vandalism encourages Fred's students to reflect seriously on the lessons learned from the experience, on the relationship between schools and the communities in which they are set, and on the role of the arts in bringing people together. Danielle reflects on what she is taking away from her study of *The Diary*: "I will try to be more kind and not be indifferent to people who are marginalized."

Although prayer isn't an appropriate response in most schools, it effectively demonstrates Fred's goals for his Catholic school students as they address their essential question: "As we bear witness to a world in which people are marginalized, forgotten, and persecuted, what

FIGURE 4.9 Students gather around the marquee after it is vandalized
Photo: James S. Chisholm.

obligations to social justice does our faith place upon us?" In it, Fred and his students take advantage of an unexpected opportunity to think about Anne Frank's message and relevance in the world today. And the students' visual, embodied, and emotional response to the vandalism reiterates their commitment to their study of Anne Frank and the Holocaust and to their community. Community members who witness the marquee's original signage, its vandalism, and its subsequent response, learn with Fred's students about the relevance of Anne Frank's message for contemporary society.

LAYERING EMOTIONAL LITERACIES

Neither a by-product of learning, nor an effect of a powerful story, or even an approach to text appreciation, *feeling the text* mediates literacy learning for students and teachers alike. In other words, feeling connects the meanings students make with the historically and culturally distant pasts and still troubled present. Creating Thick Air by feeling the firsthand testimonies of Holocaust survivors and their descendants brings Anne Frank's circumstances more to life and addresses explicitly and implicitly systemic discrimination (e.g. Mr. Gross's experience in a segregated U.S. restroom). Students use music, dance, drama, and the visual arts in Contemporary Connections to feel Anne Frank's words. Finally, students mobilize and share emotion with the broader community through Marquee, and when an opportunity emerges to reflect on the meaning of the vandalism of their school's marquee, they act as they problem solve its restoration.

Evident across these examples is the intertwining of *seeing*, *being*, and *feeling* texts. These literacies never happen in isolation; instead, they co-occur in learning contexts in which students and teachers grapple with making meanings about challenging texts in today's world. Such layering of literacies supports teachers in working with students through texts like Anne's diary, which may be unsanctioned, unfamiliar, and emotionally disturbing for different instructional environments. Classrooms can be sites for learning to make sense of challenging texts. Layering visual, embodied, and emotional literacies is an approach to promoting such learning.

Creating a community of learners is a prerequisite condition in order to teach and learn and grow in classrooms through visual, embodied, and emotional readings of challenging texts. In Chapter 5, Eileen Landay articulates arts-based principles to guide teachers and students as they build classroom communities where challenging texts can be addressed in robust ways.

REFERENCES

Beach, R., Thein, A. H., & Webb, A. (2012). *Teaching to exceed the English language arts common core state standards: A literacy practices approach to 6–12 classrooms.* New York, NY: Routledge.

Boler, M. (1999). *Feeling power.* New York, NY: Routledge.

Claxton, G. (2015). *Intelligence in the flesh: Why your mind needs your body much more than it thinks.* New Haven, CT: Yale University Press.

Eisner, E. (2002). *The enlightened eye: Qualitative inquiry and the enhancement of educational practice.* New York, NY: Macmillan.

Frank, A. (1952). *The diary of a young girl.* New York, NY: Bantam.

Gray, M. (2015). *Teaching the Holocaust: Practical approaches for ages 11–18.* New York, NY: Routledge.

Gross, F. (2010). *One step ahead of Hitler: A Jewish child's journey through France.* Macon, GA: Mercer University Press.

Karolides, N. J., & Rosenblatt, L. M. (1999). Theory and practice: An interview with Louise Rosenblatt. *Language Arts, 77*(2), 158–170.

Landay, E., & Wootton, K. (2012). *A reason to read: Linking literacy and the arts.* Cambridge, MA: Harvard Education Press.

Lewis, C., & Tierney, J. D. (2013). Mobilizing emotion in an urban classroom: Producing identities and transforming signs in a race-related discussion. *Linguistics and Education, 24*(3), 289–304.

Micciche, L. (2007). *Doing emotion.* Portsmouth, NH: Boynton/Cook Publishers.

Pahl, K., & Rowsell, J. (2010). *Artifactual literacies: Every object tells a story.* New York, NY: Teachers College Press.

Smith, F. D., & Grossman, M. (2008). *My secret camera: Life in the Łódź ghetto.* London, UK: Frances Lincoln Children's Books.

Vygotsky, L. (1986). *Thought and language* (A. Kozulin, Trans.). Cambridge, MA: The MIT Press.

Chapter 5
Begin Reading Challenging Texts by Building Community
Eileen Landay

In 1998, colleagues and I founded The ArtsLiteracy Project at Brown University. The project grew out of a desire to improve upon the everyday pedagogical practices we observed and often participated in over the years in secondary school classrooms. We brought together teachers and practicing artists with university and secondary school students to explore, try out, discuss, and document innovative approaches to teaching and learning, using methods that linked literacy and the arts. Our goal was to enrich students' learning by engaging their complete selves: heads, hands, and hearts. Our plan was to design a project around a memorable text: a poem, a play, a novel, short story, or essay; to create an essential question (McTighe & Wiggins, 2013) that addresses key issues in the text; to establish a process by which students would experience and investigate the text and the question; and then to create and present a culminating performance of understanding (Gardner, 1999). We believed that learners would be able to bring the work to life by combining and linking modalities to demonstrate their understanding in ways that were both relevant and memorable. Over a span of years, we tried out and refined these ideas working in a variety of high school, university, and professional development settings.

We wished to replace or eliminate instructional practices we considered ineffective and deeply uninteresting: the ever-present packets of worksheets that students complete and turn in to teachers, who often score them swiftly, providing a numerical grade but little actionable feedback; vocabulary word lists unconnected save for a common first letter; round robin reading in which unpracticed readers take turns publicly and painfully grappling with short portions of texts while everyone else looks on, or looks out the window; discussion formats intended to be conversations in which students offer brief—and they hope, correct—answers to teachers' "known answer" questions (Cazden, 2001). While ubiquitous, all of these practices seemed questionable to us.

We introduced an alternative curriculum that combined expressive mediums including visual art, music, dance, theater, and media arts, linking them to foundational literacies—speaking, listening, reading, and writing. We studied various approaches to arts integration, including those that expand the term literacy to multiliteracies (Kalantzis, Cope, Chan, & Dalley-Trim, 2016; New London Group, 1996) and others that emphasize transmediation, methods of enhancing learning by moving meaning making across mediums (Albers & Sanders, 2010; McCormick, 2011; Semali, 2002).

In time, a framework emerged that seemed like a sensible and practical basis for designing and implementing curriculum (see Figure 5.1). Clear, easily understood, and flexible to use, this seven-part framework has a logic that both teachers and students are able to understand and master; one that can easily be modified and adapted to a variety of settings and purposes and

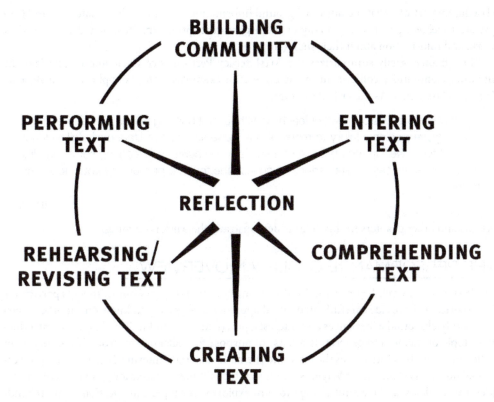

FIGURE 5.1 The Performance Cycle instructional framework
From Landay and Wootton (2012).

can readily be shared with colleagues and students. To illustrate this framework, we created a graphic that is simple and clear, yet can be elaborated with a high degree of specificity in each of its categories. We call it The Performance Cycle. (For a detailed explanation of The Performance Cycle, see Landay & Wootton, 2012, 2013.)

In 2014, colleagues and I were invited to apply The Performance Cycle model and methods in an initiative led by The Kentucky Center for the Performing Arts called Anne Frank: Bearing Witness Project, which eventually led to this book. We continue to work with teachers and students in Kentucky schools, staff, and teaching artists from The Kentucky Center, and colleagues from the University of Louisville to develop, implement, and document curriculum focused on arts-based learning opportunities that deepen understandings about the Holocaust at a personal level. Currently, nine schools across the state participate. Core texts include Anne Frank's (1952) autobiographical *The Diary of a Young Girl* and, in other classes, Lois Lowry's (1989) *Number the Stars* or Elie Wiesel's (1972) *Night*. Teaching artists support classroom teachers and include musicians, actors, writers, and visual artists as well as Holocaust survivors and children of survivors.

Participating teachers attend several gatherings and planning sessions at The Kentucky Center for the Performing Arts. Returning to their home schools, each teacher plans and implements curriculum appropriate to their setting and needs. They receive one or more visits from a teaching artist or guest speaker, as well as visits from outside observers who meet with teachers and document discussions with groups of students. Electronically, each teacher has access to

(1) a digital portfolio that includes background information and curriculum materials; and (2) a private Facebook group where many of them post descriptions, photos, or videos of student work, and information about their shared topic.

This chapter briefly summarizes the ArtsLiteracy Performance Cycle and emphasizes the Building Community component of the cycle with examples from its application in Bearing Witness classrooms. As Meier (2000) notes,

> Any time we practice our craft of teaching without first building bonds between learners, we do grave personal injury to many of our students and simultaneously fail to teach most of them well. In the absence of a safe environment, even learning something like the times tables can be subverted, much less the tougher or more rigorous academic tasks.

> (p. ix)

As this and other chapters in this volume demonstrate, the work is ongoing.

THE PERFORMANCE CYCLE: AN OVERVIEW

The Performance Cycle begins with Building Community in the classroom. Students participate in activities that provide carefully structured approaches to getting to know one another, sharing their background experiences and interests, practicing oral and written language, introducing a topic or theme, and generating a sense of purpose for collaborative work. The component called Entering Text introduces the topic and thematic material. Entering Text activities pose essential questions (McTighe & Wiggins, 2013) that focus students' attention, provide motivation, identify problems, and take initial steps toward exploring the topic and question. Comprehending Text activities that follow engage students in a rich exploration and interpretation of core texts using a variety of modalities. These activities support students' persistence, questioning, and critical thinking. In the Creating Text phase, students create personal responses to the question and topical material that involve invention and innovation in a variety of modalities. After revising and polishing their work, in Performing Text students share their learning with peers and/or a wider audience. Each step in the process provides an opportunity for contemplation and Reflection on both the work and the ongoing process.

The components of the Performance Cycle framework are not always distinct from one another. While the cycle's labels and its graphic are designed to be clear and memorable, the seven categories often overlap. Though they appear to be presented in linear steps, in practice they are often repeated as needed and in an order that best fits the circumstances. The combination of activities from the initial Building Community to final Performing Text creates a coherent overall logic that teachers and students can understand and connect with; the process establishes possibilities and purposes for studying a topic, then offers steps that enable students to move toward creating and presenting what they come to know and understand.

BUILDING A CLASSROOM COMMUNITY THROUGH THE ARTS

This chapter pays particular attention to the Building Community segment of the ArtsLiteracy Performance Cycle. James, Kathy, and I believe it's essential for you to understand the *why* and *how* of community building. To explain it, I draw on the professional literature as well as on examples from the Bearing Witness Project as it is implemented in Kentucky schools. I focus particularly on schools in addition to those featured prominently in Chapters 2–4.

As an initial step in implementing the Performance Cycle, teachers work alongside students to establish a lively and secure environment. Activities welcome and engage students, build trust, reduce boundaries, and help everyone construct and work within a well-functioning community of practice. Wenger-Trayner and Wenger-Trayner (2015) define communities of practice as "groups of people who share a concern or a passion for something they do and learn how to do it better as they interact regularly" (p. 1). Community building encourages students to be present, awake, aware, and motivated. It is designed to give them a sense that they are recognized and welcomed by others in the room and that they have thoughts, feelings, and contributions to offer the class. Both minds and bodies are engaged. Activities offer a combination of safety and challenge that help students grow toward full participation as learners and critical thinkers. Creating this environment is a crucial step and one that you'll need to revisit again and again; the students may initially be reticent—more comfortable being silent, passive, and invisible—and accustomed to working as individuals rather than as part of a collaborative community.

Community building activities take many forms, all with the purpose of creating an ensemble—the term often used in theater to express the notion of working together as a group in sync with one another. Students share experiences, create and tell one another stories, discuss in pairs and small groups, and give and receive feedback. These activities are designed to support students as they collectively address a question, revise, refine, and present together, reflect, and ultimately support each other as they create, learn, and grow (Berger, 2003; Berger, Rugen, & Woodfin, 2014). In an effective learning community built on trust and thoughtfulness, students come to feel they are in a safe space. They develop relationships and share responsibilities. Other community members take notice of who they are, take an interest in what they think and do, and provide the support they need to make choices and take risks.

Curriculum designed to introduce students to any compelling, challenging work requires that students enter an unfamiliar world, expand their learning horizons, and engage deeply. Especially when studying a topic as potentially overwhelming as the Holocaust and texts as powerful as *The Diary of a Young Girl* and *Night*, students need to *take risks, become visible, focus their attention, engage body and mind, connect with others,* and *understand and welcome purposes and routines.* Next, I describe each of these components of Building Community.

Teacher Voice Box

[Doing school usually means] the ritual of getting into class, doing whatever work is on the board, getting your materials out, being ready for the next thing. Rarely are students engaged in any kind of questions about, "How are you *really* doing today? What's happening in your life today? What's happening in other people's lives today?" That kind of listening breaks down barriers, placing the students in a better place to grow as learners.

Jane Dewey, teaching artist and program administrator

Take Risks

You'll want to begin with small steps. Even a request that students leave their seats and form a standing circle may be a challenge for some teachers in some settings, particularly if the request is unexpected. With learners' sensitivities and concerns in mind, teachers and teaching artists often begin with an activity such as Pass the Clap, where the potential for success is high and the demands relatively low. In Pass the Clap, the group forms a standing circle and a single pair turns toward one another and claps simultaneously. Then one member of the pair turns, faces a new partner and together they clap (see Figure 5.2). This turning and clapping gesture in which people receive a clap and pass it on is repeated around the entire circle. In a more challenging version, another pair starts a second clap, which may go in either the same or the opposite direction from the first. Inevitably, the claps are passed with increased speed and precision, resulting in smiles and laughter. The group has taken a first step toward becoming a community, an especially important feature of a class where important and serious work is to be undertaken.

Classroom community experiences that increase students' and teachers' risk-taking grow from the tradition of theater games (Boal, 2002; Spolin, 1983), which are known for their

FIGURE 5.2 Students in the Bearing Witness Project pass the clap
Photo: James S. Chisholm.

intention to bring groups naturally and spontaneously into drama and theater skills without effort (Spolin, 1986). (For a handbook of activities in each of the Performance Cycle categories, see the "In the Classroom" sections of chapters in Landay and Wootton (2012) and The Handbook section of the ArtsLiteracy website: www.artslit.org.)

Become Visible

During young adolescence, many students want their teachers to play a critical role in representing fairness and justice. When asked what they expect of their teachers, students describe the importance of being treated with fairness, dignity, and respect (Hattie & Yates, 2014). If they are uncertain of this treatment from either teachers or students, they often adopt a protective stance, and develop the skill of becoming invisible, not calling attention to themselves by remaining silent and as physically inconspicuous as possible.

> One experience, many of us recall, from when we were … students ourselves, is developing the art of becoming invisible. We developed skills enabling us to opt out of lesson participation. It is possible to appear slightly attentive, while avoiding direct eye gaze, avoiding excessive movement, shrinking slightly into the seat rather than sitting upright, or using bluffing tactics such as pretending to be reading or writing. It is possible to sit in a classroom, away from its focal centre, cause little disturbance, and virtually never be noticed. Observational studies have suggested this is not an uncommon experience.
>
> (Hattie & Yates, 2014, p. 47)

Even the configuration of the room in a typical middle or high school classroom lends itself to students being invisible. Seated in rows facing forward, students see one another's backs and are oriented toward the front of the room where the teacher stands. Especially in their middle-school years, and in this time in history when social media are preeminent tools for communication and identity development, students are vividly aware that one small gaff or misstep may make them the topic of ridicule leading to bullying both in person and online. By participating in activities in which they face one another and speak and move—challenging as this may be—they take the first small steps toward becoming a community in which every student is visible (Turkle, 2016).

In these small steps, students are recognized and acknowledged as individuals with names, histories, interests, and personal goals. They thrive on being recognized for their potential to contribute (Mandell & Wolf, 2001; Ritchhart, Church, & Morrison, 2011). Many of these connections involve exchanging stories that bring people to life. Early in the semester, in one Bearing Witness classroom, students leave their seats, divide into pairs, link arms, and walk together as they tell one another the story behind their names. They then retell their partners' name stories to the entire class.

The Bearing Witness Project provides an especially appropriate opportunity for teachers and students to focus on the topic of visibility and safety. The core texts, each in their own way, address this topic. Consider how, in order to survive the life-threatening world of the German occupation, it was essential for the Franks and other Jewish families to become invisible. As Anne Frank so vividly describes, her family's move into Otto Frank's company's warehouse made it possible for them to survive for over two years and for Anne to have the time and opportunity to compose her diary. Safety existed for the Frank family only by their becoming invisible and even then, only for a short while.

Focus Attention

Teaching students to become aware of and monitor their own attentional capacity is an important aspect of community building. "We are highly selective in what we pay attention to" (Hattie & Yates, 2014, p. 6) and often unaware of how our own attentional capacity works. The classic gorilla experiment makes the point vividly. Asked to watch a brief video and carefully count the number of times players pass a basketball, half of the subjects in this experiment entirely miss seeing the actor dressed in a gorilla suit, who is on-screen mugging for nearly one third of the time (Chabris & Simons, 2009; www.invisiblegorilla.com). Skillful teachers know that inattentional blindness is a characteristic of all learners' minds (Hattie & Yates, 2014). As a part of building a classroom community, you may make use of activities that call students' attention to the most important parts of the learning agenda and content and teach them to monitor and manage their own awareness.

Several kinds of activities help students build community through creating joint attention. In Blind Counting, for example, participants stand in a circle facing outward, away from one another. One person begins by saying the number "one" out loud. Another person follows by saying "two." Yet another person speaks "three." One by one, people add a number until a prearranged number is reached. The critical rule is that there are no assigned numbers; people speak as they are so moved, but no two people can speak simultaneously. If they do, the counting must begin again from one. The point is for all participants to listen to one another and to feel the energy in the room. A new group may not be able to get beyond the first few numbers, but remarkably over time, those who are inclined to speak out pull back and listen, and those who often remain silent, participate. The group improves and ultimately succeeds.

Making the essential question explicit at the outset of the study is particularly useful, especially when the question ties the topic to students' personal goals and the circumstances of their lives. In the Bearing Witness Project, for example, classrooms adopt essential questions such as "Who am I and what is my role in the community?" Emily Warne's students address the question, "How is the power of one evident in Elie Wiesel's novel, *Night*? and "How can *my* power of one impact the world?" Questions of this sort ask students to consider their roles and responsibilities to the present and to those who come after them, especially in light of what they learn in the current study.

Establishing a dual focus that connects students' personal goals to the topic of study provides a solid foundation for the work students do as the learning progresses. Some Bearing Witness students, for example, begin their studies by writing "This I Believe" essays which they present to their peers. Students in Abbey Pierce's class end their unit by writing "Letters to My Generation."

Starting a study with a focus on specific works of art is another way for students to concentrate their attention (Ritchhart et al., 2011; Yenawine, 2013). A good example is shared in Chapter 1 when Michael Schubert visits Kim Joiner's students to tell them the story of his mother, a Holocaust survivor. A cello recording of Max Bruch's *Kol Nidre* is playing in the background as the students enter. Projected on the wall before them, students see a large mural previously created by a group of high school students as part of a course called "Never Again: Nazi Germany and the Holocaust." This mural is one of a series of large-scale murals produced every year since 1992 by students in the Verbally and Mathematically Precocious Youth (V.A.M.P.Y.) summer program through the Center for Gifted Studies at Western Kentucky University. These murals, in their original form, or as photographic slides, have become a central part of the Bearing Witness Project (see Figure 5.3).

FIGURE 5.3 Michael Schubert uses a digital slide of a V.A.M.P.Y. mural as a backdrop for his story about the Holocaust

Photo: Alix Mattingly.

The uniqueness of a visiting artist in their classroom is, in itself, often enough to concentrate students' attention. Whether the visitor immediately engages them in "on your feet" activities as theater teaching artists Jane Dewey and Talleri McRae do, or beginning the class with a projected photograph and a personal story as Holocaust survivor Fred Gross does, students are immediately drawn to the themes and topics.

Teacher Voice Box

As a visiting artist, I'm very aware that I have limited time and my job is to plant as many seeds as possible. There's something about the alchemy of somebody new coming into the space that directly affects community building. A teaching artist can kickstart the energy and influence the chemistry in the room. Part of The Performance Cycle is navigating the relationship between teachers, teaching artists, and students to demonstrate how that magical triangle works together to build a community.

Talleri McRae, teaching artist

Engage Body and Mind

Being asked to leave their seats and move around when they are not expecting this kind of activity may be really challenging—even disconcerting—to students. This is not part of a pattern they are likely to have experienced over the years they have learned to "do school." In most academic settings, learning and intelligence are viewed as exclusively mental characteristics that reside entirely in the head. And while those traditional patterns certainly persist and may even have been exacerbated by the standards-and-testing emphasis of recent years, a counter-emphasis suggests that updated practices are necessary and welcome (Kalantzis et al., 2016; Landay & Wootton, 2012, 2013). The concept of *embodied cognition* is made abundantly clear when we consider the extent to which our language is built on metaphors that draw on our experience in the physical world (Lakoff & Johnson, 1980).

Increasingly, we are coming to understand the extent to which movement and gesture are integral to thinking (Claxton, 2015) and how effectively they aid learning (Goldin-Meadow & Wagner, 2005). We now know of the existence of *mirror neurons*, a distinct class of neurons in the human brain that activate as we watch others move and gesture in ways identical to the way they come to life when we move on our own. "Whether we are aware of it or not, our bodies are in a state of continual resonance with those around us," says Claxton (2015, p. 210).

> The proper substrate of the mind is not the brain alone but the entire body.... The human body (is) a massive, seething, streaming collection of interconnected communication systems that bind the muscles, the stomach, the heart, the senses and the brain so tightly together that no part—especially the brain—can be seen as functionally separate from or senior to, any other part. Torrents of electrical and chemical messages are continually coursing through the entire body and its brain.
>
> (Claxton, 2015, p. 4)

How sensible then to create events that make clear and explicit use of the body to create a common experience that lends itself to a community's understanding, particularly through the arts. For example, theater artist Talleri McRae works with high school English students to create a "living timeline," a performance portraying events in Europe leading up to and during World War II. The timeline performance is the centerpiece of a community-wide event, "A Night To Remember... Lest We Forget" held at the culmination of the project.

Gregory Acker often begins his music arts residencies with a name activity to create community and solidarity. In Kim Joiner's drama classroom, Gregory introduces students to an Indonesian bamboo shaker called the angklung because as he says, it's an "accessible way to get everyone instrumentally involved, listening to each other, learning about acoustical physics, [and] responding." He invites each student to use the rattle to create a rhythm that corresponds to her or his name and particular identities. The students present their "musical name" three times using only sound, then say their names using language. This process slows down a typically speedy task so the group can focus, and invites students to create their own rhythmic identities (see Figure 5.4).

Later in the session Gregory asks each student to choose a different instrument from the trunk that stores his collection. He challenges them to collectively create a Sound Symphony, directed by one of the students. Penelope volunteers and takes a dramatic approach to directing (see Figure 5.5).

The visual arts support connections between bodies and minds, as well. Michael Schubert visits Emily Warne's English classroom to tell the story of his mother's escape from the Holocaust. After hearing the story, students work with the visual arts to create a fabric collage that represents a young woman survivor. As Emily explains later, "Students talked about how creating that picture brought the story to life for them and helped them create a community."

FIGURE 5.4 Music educator Gregory Acker plays the angklung, an Indonesian bamboo shaker
Photo: James S. Chisholm.

FIGURE 5.5 Penelope directs a Sound Symphony with her classmates
Photo: James S. Chisholm.

Teacher Voice Box

Some of my shyest students are now the students who have branched out the most and they very much look forward to the daily arts and community building activities… I hear students say that because Ms. Warne does "this stuff," we talk much more openly around each other.

Emily Warne, English teacher

Connect with Others

In an influential analysis, Lave and Wenger (1991) theorize learning not as a set of individual cognitive processes that lead to conceptual understandings but as a set of shared social practices enacted with others in specific situations and settings. Expanding on this view, Bielaczyc and Collins (1999) identify the following key characteristics of learning communities:

- diversity of expertise among its members, who are valued for their contributions and given support to develop,
- a shared objective of continually advancing the collective knowledge and skills,
- an emphasis on learning how to learn, and
- mechanisms for sharing what is learned.

They say, "This is a radical departure from the traditional view of schooling, with its emphasis on individual knowledge and performance, and the expectation that students will acquire the same body of knowledge at the same time" (p. 2). By definition, then, an essential quality of a learning community is community members' appreciation of diversity and mutual respect.

An extensive and wide-ranging review of the education research literature makes a similar point. In a synthesis of over 800 meta-analyses that compares the efficacy of various elements of learning environments, Hattie (2009) points to the importance that classroom relationships—both teacher-to-student and peer-to-peer—have on student learning. Students show greater academic success in classrooms where teachers demonstrate respect for what each student brings to the class. They display and demonstrate listening, caring, empathy, and positive regard for their students. They convey the sense that students are capable of independent thought, that their contributions are necessary and valuable. They create conditions in which students have the power to act.

Peers too have significant influence. In early adolescence "when social relationships become particularly important … peers can assist in providing social comparisons, emotional support, social facilitation, cognitive restructuring, and rehearsal or deliberative practice" (Hattie, 2009, p. 105). Within a welcoming, supportive classroom climate, students trust both teachers and peers. They feel permission to make errors. They demonstrate concentration, persistence, and engagement.

In interviews, teachers involved in the Bearing Witness Project emphasize the importance of empathy in the middle-school years as a time when students come to see their potential for becoming productive adults and to find their way toward the positive contributions they wish to make in life. As Kelly Holland describes so well, "We can't always empathize because we haven't always been there, but we can always sympathize. We can always stop for a second and say, 'If I were in this person's shoes how would that make me feel?'" As part of James's and Kathy's research, students write definitions of empathy. Across these responses, students articulate how empathy means connecting to others by understanding and caring about others' feelings and acting on their new understandings.

To help her students think about connecting their legacy to the future, Abbey Pierce's eighth graders write "A Letter to My Generation" and present their letters to their fellow students. As their Holocaust study comes to a close, these letters are opportunities for students to express their ideas about contemporary issues like online bullying that can occur anonymously. Other students take a critical perspective toward social media platforms and some of the interpersonal consequences of being connected online all the time.

When Emily Warne assigns *The Diary of a Young Girl* or *Night* to be read as homework, she organizes an in-class activity in which students collaborate to review their literal understanding of the text. She calls this exercise, Don't Know, Sit Down. Standing in a circle, students take turns listing as many details as possible from the chapter they read as homework. One by one, students complete the sentence, "I remember...." adding something from the reading that has not already been shared. If they have no new material to share, they must sit down. Although the last person standing is declared champion, the real value is that students use their bodies as well as their minds to develop solidarity, build community, and help everyone to learn.

Teacher Voice Box

I think (students) left this unit with an understanding of how important the power of voice is... They connected the Holocaust to a lot of what they see in their daily lives with bullying, cyber bullying with social media, and other factors. This project really helped them to come together as a class and form a unit that vowed change in a generation where words, and also the lack of words, can kill. Through this project, we created an environment of empathy, action and love.

Abbey Pierce, English Language Arts teacher

Understand and Welcome Purposes and Routines

Learning communities or communities of practice are groups mutually engaged in joint activity who share a repertoire of resources (Wenger-Trayner & Wenger-Trayner, 2015). People do not simply receive, internalize, and construct knowledge as individuals, but participate in the practices of a sociocultural community with a set of structures and routines (Lave & Wenger, 1991). Under the most productive circumstances, the concept of community and a sense of purpose exist in a reciprocal relationship, one nurturing and sustaining the other.

Ideally, the adult members of the community devise and share purposes, structure, rules, and routines with the goal of making them logical, enjoyable, inspiring, motivating, and a source of learning and development to students. At the same time, individual students with their own purposes and language are likely to want to adjust and modify goals and institute changes. Teachers know this. Sometimes students will question explicitly: "Why are we doing this?" or "Why do I need to know this?" or "When will I ever use this?"

Rather than seeing these questions as cheeky or disrespectful, you might best build community in your classroom by welcoming questions and being prepared with honest answers that address goals and values students will understand and appreciate. Under the most productive circumstances, the established purposes and routines are clear and important to students, help them to focus their attention, and pique their curiosity (Willingham, 2009).

The very best curriculum projects provide an answer to the "why" question by their very nature. One obvious example is a project that serves the community beyond the classroom. Ron Berger describes how his elementary students study and report to their rural Massachusetts town on levels of radon gas in individual households and on the purity of community well water (Berger, 2003; Berger et al., 2014). He advises teachers to carry out genuine research, demonstrate standards and expectations by providing models of student work, establish a culture of feedback and critique in which students produce and improve multiple drafts of their work, and make work public.

In addition to serving the larger community, whole class projects can address and improve the sense of community among class members themselves. Greeley's (2000) description of a year in the life of her seventh-grade humanities class tells such a story. Struggling with an especially challenging group of argumentative, opinionated, and antagonistic students, Greeley wonders whether it would even be possible to undertake her customary end-of-the-year project, "building a play around the themes and content of our humanities curriculum" (p. 17). In the end, she decides to proceed and the students rise to the occasion. Both the content and the process of the original class play address what it means to build a sense of community. Greeley concludes:

> In addition to creating a climate of respect and mutual appreciation in the class, setting the bar high and giving students time to explore curriculum more deeply, we must provide students with work that itself is meaningful. All learners engage more fully in a task when they see its purpose and find some relevance to their own lives. For many students, it is essential that they see some meaning or value to the work.
>
> (p. 123)

When middle or high school students ask the "why" question about Holocaust education—and some of them are bound to wonder even if they don't ask—the answer needs to be more explicit, concrete, and personal than a generalization such as "Never Again." When studying the Holocaust, students face a particularly painful example of human beings' inhumanity to one another and address some of the hardest possible questions about the roles of conflict, morality, and social justice in human affairs.

Nothing tells us more than this story about the thin line between good and evil. Nothing shows more vividly what happens when people are socialized to consider others as less human than themselves. Nothing demonstrates more dramatically how a diary written by one young adolescent has become one of the most-read books in the world. With an examination of these topics in mind, and working within the routines established by The Performance Cycle, nothing is of greater importance and interest than this topic, the questions it raises and its potential as a source of learning for participants themselves and for the wider school community.

In one participating school, three teachers and three visiting artists work with the entire eighth grade class, and students create a series of artworks that include poetry, wooden puzzle pieces, fabric quilt squares, and written reflections, each of which represents and responds to the question: "Who are You and What is Your Place in the World?" At the culmination of the project, the art pieces hang on a cordel that rings the entire school. (The Cordel is explained in Chapter 2 and Appendix A.)

Educators who write about middle school (Balfanz, 2009; Egan, 1992; Hattie, 2009) recommend projects that "honor ... students' desire for adventure and camaraderie" and provide opportunities for short-term success in areas of strength as a foundation for building formal academic skills (Balfanz, 2009, p. 9). Purposes and routines that address these goals can be built into a schoolwide project across multiple classrooms and content areas, such as the projects undertaken above. Or they can be implemented in far more modest circumstances in a single classroom.

COMMUNITY IS A FOUNDATION FOR LEARNING

Well aware of how serious and challenging Holocaust content is, the partners in the Bearing Witness Project recognize the need to establish a strong foundation by building a sense of community within and across classrooms. Building Community activities encourage students to take risks, become visible to one another, focus their attention, engage body and mind, connect with others, and understand and welcome purposes and routines. You'll want to attend to these actions throughout any study of the Holocaust or other contemporary challenging texts. Layering visual, embodied, and emotional literacies through the arts depends on the mutual trust between teachers and their students, as well as among students themselves, cultivated in a community of learners.

Safe, fertile ground for exploring difficult topics is necessary for adolescents and their teachers to open up and share their vulnerabilities. The Performance Cycle, including creating, presenting, and reflecting on a final performance of understanding, further strengthens the community's solidarity, and an even more robust and durable foundation is established for future collaboration, learning, and growth.

In the next chapter, Renita Schmidt organizes her review of challenging picturebooks and young adult literature with an eye toward classroom activities that promote visual, embodied, and emotional literacies learning. She suggests robust pairings with *The Diary of a Young Girl* in order to address the complexity of the historical circumstances of the Holocaust and to expose contemporary genocides.

REFERENCES

Albers, P., & Sanders, J. (Eds.). (2010). *Literacies, the arts, & multimodality.* Urbana, IL: National Council of Teachers of English.

Balfanz, R. (2009). *Putting middle grades students on the graduation path: A policy and practice brief.* Westerville, OH: National Middle School Association.

Berger, R. (2003). *An ethic of excellence: Building a culture of craftsmanship with students.* Portsmouth, NH: Heinemann.

Berger, R., Rugen, L., & Woodfin, L. (2014). *Leaders of their own learning.* San Francisco, CA: Jossey-Bass.

Bielaczyc, K., & Collins, A. (1999). Learning communities in classrooms: A reconceptualization of educational practice. In C. M. Reigeluth (Ed.), *Instructional-design theories and models: A new paradigm of instructional theory* (vol. II, pp. 269–292). Mahwah, NJ: Erlbaum.

Boal, A. (2002). *Games for actors and non-actors* (2nd ed., A. Jackson, Trans.). New York, NY: Routledge.

Cazden, C. (2001). *Classroom discourse: The language of learning and teaching* (2nd ed.). Portsmouth, NH: Heinemann.

Chabris, C., & Simons, D. (2009). *The invisible gorilla: And other ways our intuitions deceive us.* New York, NY: Broadway.

Claxton, G. (2015). *Intelligence in the flesh: Why your mind needs your body much more than it thinks.* New Haven, CT: Yale University Press.

Egan, K. (1992). *Imagination in teaching and learning: The middle school years.* Chicago, IL: University of Chicago Press.

Frank, A. (1952). *The diary of a young girl.* New York, NY: Bantam.

Gardner, H. (1999). *Intelligence reframed: Multiple intelligence for the 21st century.* New York, NY: Basic Books.

Goldin-Meadow, S., & Wagner, S. M. (2005). How our hands help us learn. *Trends in Cognitive Science, 9*(5), 234–241.

Greeley, K. (2000). *"Why fly that way?" Linking community and academic achievement.* New York, NY: Teachers College Press.

Hattie, J. (2009). *Visible learning: A synthesis of over 800 meta-analyses relating to achievement.* Abingdon, UK: Routledge.

Hattie, J., & Yates, G. C. (2014). *Visible learning and the science of how we learn.* New York, NY: Routledge.

Kalantzis, M., Cope, B., Chan, E., & Dalley-Trim, L. (2016). *Literacies* (2nd ed.). New York, NY: Cambridge University Press.

Lakoff, G., & Johnson, M. (1980). *Metaphors we live by.* Chicago, IL: University of Chicago Press.

Landay, E., & Wootton, K. (2012). *A reason to read: Linking literacy and the arts.* Cambridge, MA: Harvard Education Press.

Landay, E., & Wootton, K. (2013). If walls could talk. *Educational Leadership, 70*(5), 60–64.

Lave, J., & Wenger, E. (1991). *Situated learning: Legitimate peripheral practice.* New York, NY: Cambridge University Press.

Lowry, L. (1989). *Number the stars.* New York, NY: Yearling.

Mandell, J., & Wolf, J. L. (2001). *Acting, learning and change: Creating original plays with adolescents.* Portsmouth, NH: Heinemann.

McCormick, J. (2011). Transmediation in the language arts classroom: Creating contexts for analysis and ambiguity. *Journal of Adult and Adolescent Literacy, 54*(8), 579–587.

McTighe, J., & Wiggins, G. (2013). *Essential questions: Opening doors to student understanding.* Alexandria, VA: Association for Supervision and Curriculum Development.

Meier, D. (2000). Foreword. In K. Greeley (Ed.), *"Why fly that way?" Linking community and academic achievement* (pp. ix–x). New York, NY: Teachers College Press.

New London Group. (1996). A pedagogy of multiliteracies: Designing social futures. *Harvard Educational Review, 66*(1), 60–92.

Ritchhart, R., Church, M., & Morrison, K. (2011). *Making thinking visible: How to promote engagement, understanding, and independence for all learners.* Hoboken, NJ: Wiley.

Semali, L. (Ed.). (2002). *Transmediation in the classroom: A semiotics-based media literacy framework.* Bern, Switzerland: Peter Lang.

Spolin, V. (1983). *Improvisation for the theater: A handbook of teaching and directing techniques.* Evanston, IL: Northwestern University Press.

Spolin, V. (1986). *Theater games for the classroom: A teacher's handbook.* Evanston, IL: Northwestern University Press.

Turkle, S. (2016). *Reclaiming conversation: The power of talk in a digital age.* New York, NY: Penguin.

Wenger-Trayner, E., & Wenger-Trayner, B. (2015). *Intro to communities of practice. A brief overview of the concept and its uses.* Retrieved from: http://wenger-trayner.com/introduction-to-the-communities-of-practice.

Wiesel, E. (1972). *Night.* New York, NY: Hill and Wang.

Willingham, D. T. (2009). *Why don't students like school? A cognitive scientist answers questions about how the mind works and what it means for your classroom.* Hoboken, NJ: Wiley.

Yenawine, P. (2013). *Visual thinking strategies: Using art to deepen learning across school disciplines.* Cambridge, MA: Harvard University Press.

Chapter 6
A Critical Synthesis of Picturebooks and Adolescent Literature About the Holocaust and Other Challenging Texts

Renita Schmidt

In this book, James and Kathy invite us to ponder the conceptualization of reading and teaching with challenging texts. The teachers and students who studied Anne Frank's diary and other Holocaust expository and poetic texts, primary source documents, photographs, and visuals, drew connections between their own lives and the lives of adolescents who survived the Holocaust. In this chapter I share texts and examples from my own research and work with Holocaust literature. In these contexts, I work with books that help children and young adults learn about the world and consider ethical decisions people make within human circumstances. The texts highlighted here could all be considered challenging or "tough texts" (O'Donnell-Allen, 2011) that require sensitivity and empathy from anyone who reads them, talks about them, or uses them to understand more about who they might become in the world. The ideas in this chapter and book will hopefully motivate you towards topics and contexts beyond the story of Anne Frank and the Holocaust. While I offer texts on a number of topics, most of my discussion is centered around texts related to the Holocaust; it grows from my agreement with Nodelman and Reimer's (2002) ideas about broadening notions about the construction of childhood within the context of literature for children and young adults. *A Reason to Read* (Landay & Wootton, 2012) is also an important reference point for my thinking in this chapter.

As a White middle-aged woman raised in a Christian home, I was first introduced to the horrors of the Holocaust as an adolescent when I read *The Diary of a Young Girl* (Frank, 1952). Although I am not Jewish, I have studied books about the Holocaust for the past decade (Schmidt, 2009). Everyone who studies the Holocaust needs time to study and sit quietly with texts that represent this horrific historical time. Time for talk and reflection is provided for in the seeing, being, and feeling the text activities James and Kathy share in Chapters 2–4.

Kokkola (2003) describes a path between speech and silence and the "inadequacy of language to describe, confront, and contain the Holocaust" (p. 17)—an inadequacy that often leads to silence as the only appropriate response. Kokkola, however, also argues that "dialogical silence" can be one effective way to use silence as an instrument in discussions about the Holocaust. Citing Vygotsky and Bakhtin, she reminds us that "we only know what we think by engaging in conversation with others" (p. 25), but that conversation must be followed by thinking deeply. Children of all ages need opportunities for rich discussions followed by "framed silences" or opportunities to think quietly about what was said and what was left unsaid.

PREPARING TO TEACH WITH HOLOCAUST LITERATURE

Similar to Fred Whittaker's description of introducing the Holocaust to students, when I begin a study of any new topic I often start with representations of the past around the concepts or ideas related to the topic. I find it particularly helpful to take a closer look at how time and space interact across a specific historical period. For instance, when I initiated my first study of Holocaust literature texts, I began with the term Judaism and the period in time commonly spoken of as the Holocaust. As a nonJew, I recognized I needed to expand my knowledge about Judaism from simplistic or superficial representations (e.g. food and holidays and other "tourist" notions, Derman-Sparks & Edwards, 2010). I needed to remember and learn about Jews living in many parts of the world and having many different traditions. I talked with a variety of people and discovered many secular American Jews think of their Jewishness as a matter of culture or ethnicity. The term "Jewish" is complex and multifaceted, and people define Judaism in a plethora of ways: race, culture, religion, nation, and family. Learning about Judaism was an important starting point in my first consideration of the Holocaust and what it means.

You may also feel initially underprepared to discuss Judaism as part of *The Diary of a Young Girl*. You may feel uncomfortable discussing religion in your school's context. And you may confront difficult emotions about Jewish history. Given this pedagogical context, all of the texts I discuss in this chapter fit the definition of challenging texts James and Kathy offer in Chapter 1.

The Holocaust is a challenging topic because it requires us to confront genocide and evil. The Holocaust often is a topic many teachers avoid, saying it is too personal and something that should be handled at home (Schmidt, 2009). There is no doubt that it requires serious discussion and careful consideration as a curricular topic in schools. Other tough topics or challenging texts require the same kind of care and attention; race, class, gender, and sexuality are just a few of the multifaceted, tough topics that students deserve in the school curriculum. James and Kathy address examples of such texts in Chapter 7. In the next sections, I review particular literary texts that invite learners to enter framed silences and compose multimodal responses for seeing the text, being the text, and feeling the text.

SEEING THE TEXT

Oftentimes, when we pick up a Holocaust text, we recognize the time period, setting, and topic by symbols that appear in the title or illustrations in the book. Bakhtin (1981) calls the ways real historical time and space and actual historical persons are constructed and interwoven a chronotope. For myself, a quick timeline of events is also useful to understand how chronotopes work to represent the time. Although Hitler came into power in 1933 and German laws that persecuted and segregated Jews began to be enforced from 1933 to 1938, Jews were persecuted for centuries in Europe. As Pawlikowski notes:

> When the Nazis came on the scene in Germany they were able to draw upon the legacy of Christian anti-Judaism even though biologically-based antisemitism went well beyond

classical Christian anti-Judaism by arguing for the annihilation of the Jews rather than only for their misery and marginality.

(Pawlikowski, n.d.)

During the Holocaust Jews were defined on the basis of religion by grandparents, not on affirmation of identity or religious practices.

The well-known night of terror, Kristallnacht (Night of Broken Glass), occurred in 1938 and on that evening, synagogues were set on fire and 7,000 Jewish stores in Germany were looted with 30,000 men arrested. Germany expanded the terror into Austria and Czechoslovakia in 1938, Poland in 1939, and the rest of Europe in 1940 and 1941. A particularly upsetting fact for me is the realization that six killing centers (Treblinka, Belzec, Sobibor, Auschwitz-Birkenau, Majdanek, and Chelmno) were opened in Poland in 1942 and by mid-1943, the ghettos in Poland were emptied since most Jews had been murdered that quickly. Images of prisoners in striped pajamas, Hitler, swastikas, or the words "verboten" and Kristallnacht all act as chronotopes that represent this era. We see these words as images and then quickly move to the awfulness of the Holocaust.

Picturebooks about the Holocaust provide shorter synergistic expressions of print and image for making meaning (Sipe, 2003). I use the spelling of picturebook as one word to honor that meaning making and the importance of synergy between print and image within picturebooks. Picturebooks may also help bring chronotopes to mind as you move into Cordel or Icons activities in your study (see Chapter 2). Here are several supplemental texts that might help you and your students visualize representations of the Holocaust. Figure 6.1 depicts the collection of stories I review in this chapter.

FIGURE 6.1 A collection of picturebooks and young adult literature about the Holocaust
Photo: James S. Chisholm.

The Harmonica (Johnston, 2004) is a powerful and poetic story inspired by the life of Holocaust survivor, Henryk Rosmaryn. Although the book is set in a concentration camp and very frightening, the opening pages are important. Using the voice of a survivor, Johnston begins with the words, "I cannot remember my father's face, or my mother's but I remember their love, warm and enfolding as a song." The protagonist remembers, and so the reader knows, this boy survives. This story introduces us to a family that loves Schubert and in the opening pages we meet them and see them in the beautiful pictures by illustrator Ron Mazellan. But the family is separated and the boy is sent to a different concentration camp than his parents. There his harmonica playing is very likely one of the most important reasons he survives, for the Commandant loves his ability to play Schubert.

At times, different perspectives can offer new thinking and understanding. In *Benno and the Night of Broken Glass* (Wiviott, 2010), the neighborhood cat tells the story of changes in the German and Jewish households in the days leading up to Kristallnacht. Everyone in the neighborhood shares in the care of Benno and pays loving attention to him as he comes and goes the way cats often do. Jews and Christians alike seem to live peacefully within the community until one day everything suddenly changes. For Benno, it seems people are no longer in their regular places and everyone is sad. Benno's simple perspective in a multidimensional world visible in Josée Bisaillon's illustrations, a drawn and digital montage, allows room for reflection on those terrible changes.

Likewise, *The Tree in the Courtyard* (Gottesfeld, 2016) tells the story of the Chestnut tree that grew in the courtyard of Anne Frank's hiding place. Using brown sepia ink, the illustrator, Peter McCarty, depicts a tree that can do nothing but watch as various atrocities befall the Frank family. The reader feels every emotion through the eyes of the tree, and knows that the tree lives on after the family is gone just like the Frank's actual story.

I Never Saw Another Butterfly (Volavková, 1993) is a collection of poems and drawings created by the children of Theresienstadt (also called Terezín in Czech) concentration camp. Theresienstadt was a beautiful walled city constructed by the Emperor Joseph II of Austria, approximately 60 kilometers from Prague. It was first built as a fortress with homes, taverns, a post office, a bank, a brewery, and a church. During the Second World War, however, it became a ghetto and place of deception for the Nazis. Theresienstadt was the "model camp" shown as a place to "sit out the war safely and quietly." Although the adults there soon knew it as an entirely false place where they waited to be transported to a death camp, the children knew nothing about the fate that awaited them. Although everyone in this camp was locked in and children were often asked to work like adults, they maintained a childish outlook and secretly studied and drew pictures. On one hand, they saw things most children never see—long lines to obtain food, executions, and profane expressions in a combination of languages. On the other hand, they somehow also continued to see the beauties of the world around them—green meadows, bluish hills, animals, birds, and butterflies. *Fireflies in the Dark* (Rubin, 2000), *The Cat with the Yellow Star* (Rubin, 2006), and *Terezín: Voices from the Holocaust* (Thomson, 2011) are excellent companion texts to *I Never Saw Another Butterfly*.

Finally, *Rose Blanche* (Gallaz & Innocenti, 1985) is the story of a German girl by the same name. The story title is a nod to the German resistance movement White Rose, which was a multi-city, student-driven resistance movement that denounced the Nazi regime and whose leaders were eventually executed. As the story opens, we see that German soldiers have arrived in the town and appear to be taking over. One day, Rose sees a boy taken away by the German soldiers, so she follows the path of the truck out into the woods. She walks farther into the forest than she has ever gone before and in the clearing of the forest, she finds people surrounded by a barbed wire fence. You and other readers will recognize it as a concentration camp. Rose begins to bring food to the children in the camp, but one day when she arrives she finds the people gone. Soldiers quickly surround Rose who has become the enemy. Innocenti's watercolor illustrations contribute significantly to the vivid images (Whitmore & Crowell, 1994). A meaningful companion book to *Rose Blanche* is *We Will Not Be Silent: The White Rose Student Resistance Movement that Defied Adolf Hitler* (Freedman, 2016).

In thinking about helping students make meaning through image in Holocaust texts, I thought also about titles that deal with current challenging topics. In the graphic novel *Drowned City* (Brown, 2016), for example, Don Brown's drawings take us right into the center of Hurricane Katrina and the despair of the people who could not get out of New Orleans when the storm hit. The book sheds light on the complexity and scope of this horrific event and offers powerful material for critical literacy discussions about societal privilege and responsibility to others. *How It Went Down* (Magoon, 2014) is another text that deals with the all-too-familiar shooting of an innocent black teenager by a vigilant passerby. In eighteen different voices, the reader is provided with a compelling look at who we are versus who we want to be or are pressured to become. Be aware that this book contains prolific use of profanity.

BEING THE TEXT

Bringing words to life through voice, movement, gesture, and actions is another important way to bring meaning to challenging texts. In an after-school book club I co-direct on Friday afternoons with fourth- to sixth-grade girls (Thein & Schmidt, 2017), the girls often ask to dramatize, draw, and even write about what is happening in the texts we read together. Sometimes girls tell their own stories that are similar to what has happened to a character in a text we read, or they dramatize the characters' stories, spontaneously adding gestures and movement as part of their everyday storytelling practices. In this section, I describe several texts that can help you encourage transmediation (Siegel, 1995) and performative responses (Sipe, 2002) that build critical thinking and being the text.

Beginning with the plethora of stories on Anne Frank, hiding has become an almost romanticized way of teaching about the Holocaust. Stories of occupation and hiding abound in the literature related to the Holocaust, especially in stories about the resistance efforts of nonJews living during the time. I recommend approaching stories like this with caution. For instance, *The Lily Cupboard* (Oppenheim, 1992) depicts a young Jewish girl named Miriam and her father driving to the idyllic countryside represented in watercolor paintings by Ronald Himler. The story continues as a heroic Dutch family hides Miriam in the secret lily cupboard off the kitchen that will keep her safe if the soldiers come. It is important to think about the feeling of a child who is old enough to understand the need to hide and the terror she must have faced when she heard "Frère Jacque," the song that acted as her cue to hide. Adolescents reading this story might also think about the agony of sending a child away to hide and the constant worry that the family and child would remain safe during the numerous raids that occurred across the countryside.

Twenty and Ten (Bishop, 1952) is another story that takes place in France during the German occupation in World War II. It is illustrated in ink drawings by William Pène du Bois. Twenty French children who have been sent to the countryside for safety help protect and hide ten Jewish refugee children when the Nazis come looking for them. While this is the story of French

Christians hiding Jewish children, most interesting is the narrative structure of the story. In the story, Claire Hutchet Bishop invokes the idea that children often only have partial understanding of situations and gives the storyline playful moments that enable the children to outfox Nazi soldiers and successfully hide the Jewish children who are living with them. Unfortunately, there is a definite feeling in this book that the Catholic French children are saving the Jewish victims. Jews as victims is a common theme in children's literature. As you will notice, the Jewish children in the text are silent. You could, however, encourage your students to consider the voices that are silent and bring them meaningful words that show their strength and resilience during a terrible ordeal.

It is important and critical to consider silence with all texts. When characters in books are silent, the reader should ask why. For *Twenty and Ten*, written in 1952, this may be directly related to the cultural norms of the time in children's literature. Issues of power and authority and cultural sensitivity were not often addressed in works for children written during that decade.

In *The Girl in the Blue Coat* (Hesse, 2016), Hanneke spends her days searching for the black-market goods her neighbors want and need in 1943 Amsterdam, Netherlands. She engages in this dangerous work as a response to her boyfriend's death on the frontlines and as a way to actively contribute to the war effort. Her parents feel concerned about her odd hours of work at a funeral parlor and she hides her black-market work from them and her friends, many of whom believe her work is unethical. Hanneke's family needs the money she makes, however. When Mrs. Janssen, one of her customers, asks her to help find a missing young girl she had been hiding in her pantry, Hanneke discovers some of her friends are members of a resistance movement and they lead her into espionage and terror in her efforts to solve the mystery of the vanished girl in the blue coat.

Finally, *The Yellow Star*, written by Carmen Agra Deedy and illustrated by Henri Sørenson (2000), is a picturebook based on a legend or myth about King Christian of Denmark. In this book, the story is told of King Christian asking every Dane to wear the yellow star so it is impossible to discriminate between Jews and nonJews in Copenhagen. While the story of the yellow star and how it was used to represent Jews during WWII provides background knowledge for students who do not know what the yellow star signified, the story is legend, a myth, that is too often taken as truth. In telling this story as a tale of myth rather than truth, the silence of Jewish voices in the text can be reconsidered and possibly voiced as students more deeply understand the plot to fool the Nazi soldiers.

As I think about contemporary literature, I recognize that our world continues to shrink every day with more and more people traveling and immigrating to new countries while racial profiling escalates in the United States. Now more than ever, it is crucial to consider ways to build understanding across cultures and ethnicities. *Watched* (Budhos, 2016) is a contemporary story of a Bangladeshi Muslim teen named Naeem who lives in New York City. When he is unfairly accused of shoplifting, the police offer him asylum if he will work for them and spy on his own family, friends, and neighbors. Naeem shows great courage and in the face of fear he defies the police and becomes active in his cousin's resistance organization.

Too often, voices and stories are silent or never told. Consider reading texts that offer other perspectives as you work with students to embody the text. Untold stories about African Americans are available in *Voices from the March on Washington* (2014), by poets J. Patrick Lewis and George Ella Lyon, and *Freedom in Congo Square* (2016), written by Carole Boston Weatherford and illustrated by R. Gregory Christie. Weatherford's words and Christie's folk art illustrations provide a new perspective on how enslaved persons expressed emotion through the arts of music and dance on Sunday in contrasting relief to the toil of the rest of the days of the week. In a more contemporary untold story, *My Story, My Dance* (2015), Lesa Cline-Ransome's language emphasizes poetically details of Robert Battle's journey to the Alvin Ailey Dance Company, after wearing a brace on his leg for most of his childhood. James Ransome's illustrations portray the dancer's movement with precision and guide readers' attention to the body.

Margarita Engle is a Cuban-American author who has written several recent stories from the perspective of the voices that are often silenced. *Drum Dream Girl* (2015), illustrated by Rafael López, is the story of a Cuban girl who worked diligently to become one of the first female percussionists in Cuban history. *Silver People* (2014) takes you to the building of the Panama Canal through the voices of the animals in the jungle, a young Cuban worker, and a medicine woman who sells herbal medicines to the men who work on the canal.

FEELING THE TEXT

Rosenblatt (1978) argues that readers experience efferent and aesthetic responses during engaged reading experiences. Lewis (2000) extends Rosenblatt's thinking and reminds us that every text is political and students are capable of having critical transactional responses to texts especially when voices are missing or silenced or completely absent within a text. In this last section, I take up some of the critical reading and response that is important when working with challenging texts related to the Holocaust. Feeling the text is a literacy practice that helps students transform and build what Freire (1970) calls "conscientization," or critical consciousness.

Several picturebooks tell the story of a Polish doctor named Janusz Korczak who cared for Jewish children whose parents were incarcerated or killed during the Holocaust. In *A Hero and the Holocaust* (2002), author David Adler and illustrator Bill Farnsworth tell the story of Dr. Korczak who studied to be a doctor and started an orphanage for Jewish children. Another picturebook, *The Champion of Children* (Bogacki, 2009), includes the famous canary story from Korczak's childhood to emphasize the idea that being Jewish set him apart early in his life. By the time he attended university, he knew he would devote his life to children and he studied medicine to accomplish this. He founded an orphanage in which children governed themselves and created a weekly newspaper. In *Mister Doctor* (2015), written by Irène Cohen-Janca and illustrated by Maurizio A. C. Quarello, we learn that when the Nazis invaded Poland, Korczak moved with the children into the ghetto where he continued to watch over them and began to keep his famous Ghetto Diary. He died with the children in the Treblinka death camp. His work was a testament to his dedication to critical consciousness.

Children were also important in the resistance movement during the Holocaust. Bartoletti wrote two texts that explain Hitler's concerted efforts at seducing children into the Nazi movement: *Hitler Youth* (2005) and *The Boy Who Dared* (2008). Hitler Youth was one of the largest clubs for adolescents and Hitler knew the road to success for his ideas could come through young people. This nonfiction book contains numerous photographs. The book centers on twelve boys and girls who were members of the Hitler Youth. Some spied and did harm, but others were resistant. *The Boy Who Dared* is the story of a brave German boy named Helmuth who was immediately attracted by the uniforms and bravado of the Nazi Stormtroopers. His thinking changed as he began to realize what was really happening and that the government was lying to the people of Germany.

In contemporary connections, students will also likely be drawn to discussions about immigration and the plight of refugees in the current political climate. A picturebook called *Two White Rabbits* (2015), written by Jairo Buitrago and illustrated by Rafael Yockteng, describes the dangerous journey of escape through the eyes of a young girl traveling with her father on the train called The Beast. One has to wonder what would compel a parent to risk everything, life itself, and ride the rails across Mexico on the back of this terrifying train. (See Chapter 7 for a paired text for this book: *Enrique's Journey*.) Reading this child's story is a compelling first step to awareness, understanding, and compassion about the realities of being a refugee. Likewise, *Stepping Stones: A Refugee Family's Journey* (Ruurs, 2016) introduces us to Rama and her family as they flee the civil war near their home and set off on foot for Europe carrying as many belongings as possible on their backs. The beautiful stone illustrations by Syrian artist, Nizar Ali Bardr, inspired the author, Margriet Ruurs to write this compelling story told in English and Arabic.

Too often we misunderstand cultures, people, and their stories. Some other texts that might help students consider untold perspectives are *Balcony on the Moon* (Barakat, 2016), the memoir of Ibtisam Barakat's life growing up in Palestine from 1972 to 1981 under Israeli occupation and persecution, and *Every Falling Star* (Lee & McClelland, 2016), the memoir of a young North Korean defector named Sungju Lee. The resilience and perseverance of the people in these stories will bring strong emotions into your discussions. Ruta Sepetys (2016) offers *Salt to the Sea* for a close look at four fictional characters from East Prussia, Poland, and the Baltic countries who learn to trust one another despite the prejudices they have established during World War II.

LAYERING LITERACIES FOR CRITICAL MEANING MAKING

Using a variety of print materials, such as poetry, drama, newspapers, comic books, graphic novels, children's and young adult literature, and non-print materials like images, music, video, and other digital sources, will play an important role in layering literacies for deep meaning making in your classroom. Providing children with multiple genres broadens perspectives on complex topics, and time spent reading builds knowledge about the world.

I invite you to consider these questions:

- How do we reach students' emotions?
- How do we cultivate sensitivity, compassion, and empathy?
- How old must readers be to make the distinction between violence presented in the media and historical violence taught in the classroom?

An important undertaking for you will be planning response engagements with reading materials that encourage critical thinking through personal connections. With foundations in sociocultural theory, critical literacy considers the ways texts are constructed within social, political, and historical contexts and how these contexts position readers (Comber & Simpson, 2001). Cope and Kalantzis's (2000) concept of multiliteracies and the work of sociocultural scholars who theorize situated literacy learning (Barton, Hamilton, & Ivanič, 2000; Kress, 2003; Street, 1995) emphasize a critical perspective while contextualizing literacy in multiple modes and media. This work is also grounded in the transactional theory of reader response as described by Rosenblatt (1978), in which readers construct unique meaning based on individual experiences and perceptions. Since all texts represent particular cultural positions and discourses, text sets that reflect different perspectives may also be regarded as a way to invite students to engage in critical discussions of complex issues in the world and the relationship between language and power (Leland, Lewison, & Harste, 2013).

In Appendix B you'll find a list of high quality books that I recommend for children's and adolescents' study of the Holocaust. In Appendix C, James, Kathy, and I provide a list of additional books that may be helpful in your pursuit for deep understanding with challenging texts. Next, in Chapter 7, James and Kathy return to consider three specific contemporary challenging texts and offer teaching practices that support students' multimodal meaning making with them.

REFERENCES

Adler, D. A. (2002). *A hero and the Holocaust: The story of Janusz Korczak and his children.* Illus. B. Farnsworth. New York, NY: Holiday House.

Bakhtin, M. M. (1981). *The dialogic imagination: Four essays by M.M. Bakhtin* (M. Holquist, Ed.; C. Emerson & M. Holquist, Trans.). Austin, TX: University of Texas Press.

Barakat, I. (2016). *Balcony on the moon.* New York, NY: Farrar, Straus and Giroux.

Bartoletti, S. C. (2005). *Hitler youth: Growing up in Hitler's shadow.* New York, NY: Scholastic.

Bartoletti, S. C. (2008). *The boy who dared.* New York, NY: Scholastic Press.

Barton, D., Hamilton, M., & Ivanič, R. (2000). *Situated literacies: Reading and writing in context.* New York, NY: Routledge.

Bishop, C. H. (1952). *Twenty and ten.* Illus. W. P. du Bois. New York, NY: Scholastic.

Bogacki, T. (2009). *The champion of children: The story of Janusz Korczak.* New York, NY: Francis Foster Books.

Brown, D. (2016). *Drowned city: Hurricane Katrina & New Orleans.* New York, NY: Houghton Mifflin Harcourt.

Budhos, M. (2016). *Watched.* New York, NY: Wendy Lamb Books.

Buitrago, J. (2015). *Two white rabbits.* Illus. R. Yockteng. Toronto, ON: Groundwood Press.

Cline-Ransome, L. (2015). *My story, my dance: Robert Battle's journey to Alvin Ailey.* New York, NY: Simon & Schuster.

Cohen-Janca, I. (2015). *Mister doctor: Janusz Korczak and the orphans of the Warsaw ghetto* (P. Ayer, Trans.). Illus. M. A. C. Quarello. Toronto, ON, Canada: Annick Press.

Comber, B., & Simpson, A. (Eds.). (2001). *Negotiating critical literacies in classrooms.* New York, NY: Routledge.

Cope, B., & Kalantzis, M. (Eds.). (2000). *Multiliteracies: Literacy learning and the design of social futures.* New York, NY: Routledge.

Deedy, C. A. (2000). *The yellow star: The legend of King Christian X of Denmark.* Illus. H. Sørensen. Atlanta, GA: Peachtree.

Derman-Sparks, L., & Edwards, J. O. (2010). *Anti-bias education for young children and ourselves.* Washington, DC: National Association for the Education of Young Children.

Engle, M. (2014). *Silver people: Voices from the Panama Canal.* New York, NY: Houghton Mifflin Harcourt.

Engle, M. (2015). *Drum dream girl: How one girl's courage changed music.* Illus. R. López. New York, NY: Houghton Mifflin Harcourt.

Frank, A. (1952). *The diary of a young girl.* New York, NY: Bantam.

Freedman, R. (2016). *We will not be silent: The white rose student resistance movement that defied Adolf Hitler.* New York, NY: Clarion.

Freire, P. (1970). *Pedagogy of the oppressed.* New York, NY: Continuum.

Gallaz, C., & Innocenti, R. (1985). *Rose Blanche.* Illus. R. Innocenti. Mankato, MN: Creative Editions.

Gottesfeld, J. (2016). *The tree in the courtyard: Looking through Anne Frank's window.* Illus. P. McCarty. New York, NY: Knopf.

Hesse, M. (2016). *The girl in the blue coat.* Boston, MA: Little, Brown and Company.

Johnston, T. (2004). *The harmonica.* Illus. R. Mazellan. Watertown, MA: Charlesbridge.

Kokkola, L. (2003). *Representing the Holocaust in children's literature.* New York, NY: Routledge.

Kress, G. (2003). *Literacy in the new media age.* Abingdon, UK: Routledge.

Landay, E., & Wootton, K. (2012). *A reason to read: Linking literacy and the arts*. Cambridge, MA: Harvard Education Press.

Lee, S., & McClelland, S. E. (2016). *Every falling star*. New York, NY: Harry N. Abrams.

Leland, C., Lewison, M., & Harste, J. (2013). *Teaching children's literature: It's critical!* New York, NY: Routledge.

Lewis, C. (2000). Critical issues: Limits of identification: The personal, pleasurable and critical in reader response. *Journal of Literacy Research, 32*(2), 253–266.

Lewis, J. P., & Lyon, G. E. (2014). *Voices from the march on Washington*. New York, NY: Boyds Mills/ WordSong.

Magoon, K. (2014). *How it went down*. New York, NY: Henry Holt.

Nodelman, P., & Reimer, M. (2002). *The pleasures of children's literature* (3rd ed.). New York, NY: Pearson.

O'Donnell-Allen, C. (2011). *Tough talk, tough texts: Teaching English to change the world*. Portsmouth, NH: Heinemann.

Oppenheim, S. L. (1992). *The lily cupboard*. Illus. R. Himler. New York, NY: HarperCollins.

Pawlikowski, J. T. (n.d.). *Introduction to Gerald S. Sloyan's article on Christian persecution of Jews over the centuries*. Retrieved from: www.ushmm.org/research/the-center-for-advanced-holocaust-studies/ programs-ethics-religion-the-holocaust/articles-and-resources/christian-persecution-of-jews-over-the-centuries

Rosenblatt, L. (1978). *The reader, the text, the poem: The transactional theory of the literary work*. Carbondale: Southern Illinois University Press.

Rubin, S. G. (2000). *Fireflies in the dark: The story of Friedl Dicker-Brandeis and the children of Terezin*. New York, NY: Holiday House.

Rubin, S. G. (2006). *The cat with the yellow star: Coming of age in Terezin*. New York, NY: Holiday House.

Ruurs, M. (2016). *Stepping stones: A refugee family's journey* (F. Raheem, Trans.). Illus. A. Bardr. Victoria, BC: Orca Press.

Schmidt, R. (2009). Finding our way with teachers and families: Reading and responding to the Holocaust. In K. M. Leander, D. W. Rowe, D. K. Dickinson, M. K. Hundley, R. T. Jiménez, & V. J. Risko (Eds.), *58th yearbook of the national reading conference* (pp. 248–260). Oak Creek, WI: National Reading Conference.

Sepetys, R. (2016). *Salt to the sea*. New York, NY: Philomel Books.

Siegel, M. (1995). More than words: The generative power of transmediation for learning. *Canadian Journal of Education, 20*(4), 455–475.

Sipe, L. R. (2002). Talking back and taking over: Young children's expressive engagement during story-book read-alouds. *The Reading Teacher, 55*(5), 476–483.

Sipe. L. R. (2003). How picturebooks work: A semiotically framed theory of text-picture relationships. *Children's Literature in Education, 29*(2), 97–108.

Street, B. (1995). *Social literacies: Critical approaches to literacy in development, ethnography and education*. New York, NY: Longman.

Thein, A. H., & Schmidt, R. R. (2017). Challenging, rewarding emotion work: Critical witnessing in an after-school book club. *Language Arts, 94*(5), 313–325.

Thomson, R. (2011). *Terezín: Voices from the Holocaust*. Somerville, MA: Candlewick Press.

Volavková, H. (Ed.). (1993). *I never saw another butterfly: Children's drawings and poems from Terezin concentration camp, 1942–1944*. New York, NY: Schocken Books.

Weatherford, C. B. (2016). *Freedom in Congo Square*. Illus. G. Christie. New York, NY: Little Bee Books.

Whitmore, K. F., & Crowell, C. G. (1994). *Inventing a classroom: Life in a bilingual, whole language learning community*. York, ME: Stenhouse Publishers.

Wiviott, M. (2010). *Benno and the night of the broken glass*. Illus. J. Bisaillon. Minneapolis, MN: Kar-Ben Publishing.

Chapter 7
Layering Literacies with Other Challenging Texts

This book highlights how teachers and students read challenging texts by moving their meaning-making practices across expressive, arts-based mediums. We suggest that this process, which we call layering literacies through the arts, deepens students' complex thinking and elevates engagement. In Chapters 2–4, we show how eighth-grade students engage in arts-based instructional strategies as they move from reading Anne Frank's (1952) words in *The Diary of a Young Girl* to:

- *seeing* the personal and historical context in which she wrote, using Cordel, Icons, and Archives to layer visual texts;
- *being* the text to freeze moments in *The Diary* through embodied gestures during Tableau and Pantomime, Sculpture Garden, and Dramatic and Staged Performances; and
- *feeling* the text by creating and sustaining a classroom atmosphere rich with emotion related to past- and present-day injustices via Creating Thick Air, Contemporary Connections, and Marquee.

In Chapter 5, Eileen Landay emphasizes the importance of Building Community in classrooms in which risk-taking and storytelling can take place, so that students can feel safe reading and engaging with challenging texts. In Chapter 6, Renita Schmidt widens and deepens our knowledge about the range of high quality literature about the Holocaust and other challenging picturebooks and young adult literary texts.

In this book, Anne Frank's diary serves as the primary example of a challenging text. Anne's story often functions as the introduction to the Holocaust for middle grades students and her diary has canonical status in U.S. middle schools and around the world. Yet, *The Diary* regularly makes the list of most frequently banned books because it contains "inappropriate" content for middle school classrooms. Objections to the use of *The Diary* in curricula cite "offensive … sexual content" and point to passages of Anne's diary in which she is writing about her body and her "discovery of intimate feelings" (Abramovitch, 2012, pp. 174–176).

Anne's diary is a challenging text, too, due to the content knowledge required to contextualize her writing. For even the most historically well-informed teacher, there will likely be related to Anne's diary historical, religious, linguistic, and cultural knowledge that is unfamiliar.

Finally, *The Diary* is a challenging text because its historical context is the Nazi genocide of 6 million Jews and millions of others during World War II. In other words, one can't arguably teach students and learn with students from Anne Frank's diary without contextualizing the work in its emotionally troubling history—a history about which scholars and descendants of perpetrators, resisters, bystanders, victims, and survivors continue to discover new information.

All three of the criteria we use to conceptualize challenging texts are especially important in *The Diary* due to the unresolvable nature of the questions it generates about the Holocaust and humanity. In other words, the questions we have at the end of our study are not likely to be resolved the next time we read Anne's diary with our students. These criteria for challenging texts—unsanctioned, potentially unfamiliar, and emotionally troubling content—should, however, not be grounds for exclusion from the curriculum. Rather, we argue that through the arts teachers and students engage in rich interpretive work by drawing on diverse modes of expression and accessing emotion as a resource to bridge unfamiliar content.

In this chapter, we extend the practice of layering literacies through the arts with three additional books that we consider to be challenging texts. We aim to demonstrate the versatility and adaptability of the arts-based strategies described in Chapters 2–4 for use with this contemporary literature. We feel arts-based strategies that invite students to see, be, and feel the text have potential for disrupting dominant and normative perspectives about race, gender, class, sexuality, immigration, violence, and other difficult (Britzman, 1998), complex topics. Arts-based strategies with challenging literature, taken as a whole, can be entry points for classroom learning about social problems and increasing critical consciousness. They initiate classroom conversations that build readers' capacities to engage in civil discourse, what O'Donnell-Allen (2011) describes as "conversations that matter—the kind authors have with their readers, readers have with other readers, and all of us as citizens have with one another" (p. 6).

As the chapter proceeds, we share brief synopses for three books. We explore seeing the text with Sherman Alexie's (2007) *The Absolutely True Diary of a Part-Time Indian*, being the text with Sharon Flake's (1998) *The Skin I'm In*, and feeling the text with Sonia Nazario's (2013) *Enrique's Journey: The True Story of a Boy Determined to Reunite with His Mother (Adapted for Young People)*. We identify the potential reasons reading these texts in classrooms might be challenging and we illustrate ways in which the arts can be used to enact and layer powerful literacies learning opportunities for students. Finally, we provide additional resources to use when teaching students with each book. We remind you about Appendix A where you will find specific classroom instructions for carrying out the arts-based strategies we describe here and elsewhere in the book. Although we demonstrate how each book lends itself to seeing, being, or feeling the text, we acknowledge that each book can—and should—be approached using a combination of visual, embodied, and emotional arts-based strategies.

We make a few disclaimers here prior to discussing these compelling books. First, what makes any text challenging is always dependent on the sociocultural context in which people read that text. Some readers might never imagine that one of the books we review below might be unsanctioned, unfamiliar, or emotionally troubling in terms of content. And still other readers might immediately want to dismiss that same book as "impossible" to teach in a given school setting. We argue, along with a number of literary award-granting bodies, that these are rich and compelling texts, but perhaps even more important for our purposes, that these books can promote the kinds of critical conversations that our society, indeed our humanity, needs at this historical moment (Hess & McAvoy, 2015; O'Donnell-Allen, 2011).

Finally, we want to share our thinking as we selected books for this chapter. First, all are well known and readily available, and will be familiar to many prospective and practicing English Language Arts teachers and readers of children's and young adult literature. Second, these texts feature strong and complex protagonists or figures like Anne Frank whose perspectives, feelings, fears, and hopes were not inhibited throughout the narrative. Third, we chose texts for which essentializing others, or reducing and attributing as "natural" to individuals typically stereotypical characteristics of an entire group, is complicated by the intersections of race, gender, identity, sexuality, ethnicity, and immigration status embodied in the characters (real and fictional) we meet in these books. And finally, we include books that fit especially well the criteria we used to characterize Anne Frank's diary as challenging. All of the books below might contain unsanctioned school content (e.g. sexual themes, violence), content that is unknown or unfamiliar to some teachers (e.g. indigenous cultural activities and ceremonies, intraracism), and situations that are emotionally troubling (deportation, acknowledging one's privilege). Of course, there are many brilliantly crafted narratives that could have been included below and we welcome readers to integrate those texts, too, within the arts-based, layering literacies approach we outline in this book. We offer help in this regard with a bibliography of recommended challenging texts in Appendix C.

SEEING THE TEXT WITH *THE ABSOLUTELY TRUE DIARY OF A PART-TIME INDIAN*

Sherman Alexie's (2007) *The Absolutely True Diary of a Part-Time Indian* is a critically acclaimed young adult novel that has been recognized for its hilarious and heartbreaking depiction of Arnold Spirit, Jr., a young man who decides to leave his Spokane Indian reservation to attend a White high school some twenty miles away. Evident in Alexie's title, Arnold, in addition to navigating many of the coming-of-age experiences portrayed in typical young adult texts (Buehler, 2016), must also negotiate his own identities as a member of the Spokane Indian reservation and as the only ninth-grade American Indian student in an all-White school. The image of Arnold's bifurcated self is conveyed through Arnold's self-doubt, self-deprecating humor, and biting wit. The splitting of Arnold's identities is further explored through "his own" sketches throughout the book. Artist Ellen Forney's images, in fact, present a parallel narrative that provides graphic insight into Arnold's character, with all of its emotional, social, and psychological features. Arnold's strained relationship with his best friend, Rowdy, creates the narrative space within which Arnold can communicate how he feels constantly pulled both physically and figuratively toward Wellpinit, his reservation home, and Rearden, his adopted home. This tension is left unresolved over the course of the novel as Arnold is dealt one devastating loss after another. Yet, his reuniting with Rowdy, in the end, offers a glimmer of hope for Arnold amidst a sea of challenges, as Arnold comes to terms with himself and his future.

There are many features of this book that fit the criteria we present for challenging texts. Teachers may not have experience or background knowledge about American Indian reservations, their histories, cultures, and geographic locations. Alexie introduces the reader to the Bureau of Indian Affairs, powwow celebrations, and the Indian Health Service—all potentially unfamiliar to teachers. Additionally, the novel is emotionally devastating. Arnold experiences, for example, the deaths of his grandmother, his father's best friend, and his sister. The toll of these deaths on Arnold is mitigated through the protagonist's humor and matter-of-fact reflections on their meanings.

More than any other criterion, however, *The Absolutely True Diary of a Part-Time Indian* is a challenging text because it features on almost every one of its more than 200 pages taboo, unsanctioned, and often off-limits topics for study in school. The following is only a partial list of topics Alexie takes up provocatively and expertly: medical issues and conditions, depression, masturbation, incarceration, profanity, poverty, alcoholism, violence, death, and racism.

Rather than avoid *The Absolutely True Diary of a Part-Time Indian* because of these challenges, we, and many readers, including teachers and students, are drawn to this text by these issues, especially given a portrayal of them by Alexie that is honest, unflinching, and reads so genuinely. Crandall (2009), for example, takes up Arnold's medical condition as an unsanctioned topic in school in order to argue for the usefulness of the young adult novel in disrupting binary thinking about able and disabled bodies as he explores medical and socially constructed readings of Arnold's disability:

> Blaming the individual for a disability (in Arnold's case, being an Indian with hydrocephalus) and mandating they adapt to normal society (in this case, American society) is different than blaming society for how an individual with a disability or who is from a particular culture is accepted.
>
> (p. 73)

Crandall (2009) shows how productive readings of challenging texts emerge when taboo topics are highlighted rather than hidden in the classroom. We present next resources and illustrations for ways in which teachers and students might broach other critical dialogues that this novel ultimately provokes.

Arts-based Strategies for Seeing the Text

> If you speak and write in English, or Spanish, or Chinese, or any other language, then only a certain percentage of human beings will get your meaning. But when you draw a picture, everybody can understand it... So I draw because I want to talk to the world. And I want the world to pay attention to me.
>
> —Arnold Spirit, Jr. (Alexie, 2007, pp. 5–6)

Arnold teaches us through his reflections about the power of the visual text to communicate his identities. Additionally, Fornay's illustrations and the intense imagery in the book compel us to approach instruction with Alexie's semi-autobiographical narrative through arts-based strategies that encourage students to see the text. Not unlike Kim Joiner's approach with *The Diary of a Young Girl*, think about the use of the cordel to orient student readers to the places where Arnold Spirit, Jr.'s story plays out. A cordel that introduces Alexie's novel might include multimodal texts like the following (Figure 7.1):

- brief, yet powerful quotations from Arnold that convey some of the issues taken up in the narrative;
- graphical representations of socioeconomic realities that impact the Spokane Indian reservation;
- census data;
- other works by Alexie, including "Powwow Polaroid" (1998);
- a timeline of American Indian history;
- illustrations from the novel; and
- maps that depict the Spokane Indian reservation at different historical moments.

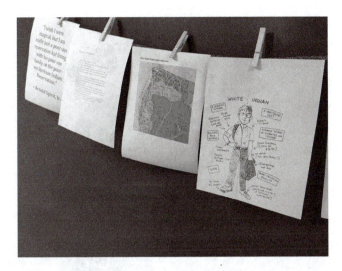

FIGURE 7.1 A cordel to introduce *The Absolutely True Diary of a Part-Time Indian*
Photo: James S. Chisholm.

After students select these texts from the cordel, they engage in inquiry around them. Teachers might ask students, for example, to describe the changes they see in the maps that represent the Spokane Indian reservation over time; identify any trends they see in the census data; provide preliminary linguistic or visual interpretations of Alexie's (1998) "Powwow Polaroid"; dramatize quotations and sketches pulled from the novel; or investigate in more depth various moments on the American Indian history timeline. All of these options promote student choice and provide support for students to "analyze and understand the politics of difference and struggle" (Talbert, 2012, p. 266).

Icons is another way to help students see the text. With this novel, Icons can help students access and deepen the concept of poverty, particularly as it impacts Arnold throughout the narrative. Arnold's descriptions of the poverty that surrounds his family are vivid. He says:

- "I wish I were magical, but I am just a poor-ass reservation kid living with his poor-ass family on the poor-ass Spokane Indian Reservation" (p. 7).
- "Do you know the worst thing about being poor? Oh, maybe you've done the math in your head and you figure:
  Poverty = empty refrigerator + empty stomach" (p. 8).
- "Poverty doesn't give you strength or teach you lessons about perseverance. No, poverty only teaches you how to be poor" (p. 13).

Students might create icons of the textbook Arnold received in school, which was the same textbook his mother used (it included her maiden name on the inside cover) when she attended the reservation school, making the textbook at least 30 years older than Arnold. They might create abstract visual representations of the role of poverty in Arnold's life by depicting his blistered feet that resulted from walking the 20 plus miles to school when he couldn't hitchhike a ride (see Figure 7.2). Because there are so many moments in the novel when Arnold's poverty confronts the reader, a classroom of students may all choose different icons without repeating any one depiction—a startling testimony both to Arnold's strength in the face of hardship and the socioeconomic devastation endured in his community.

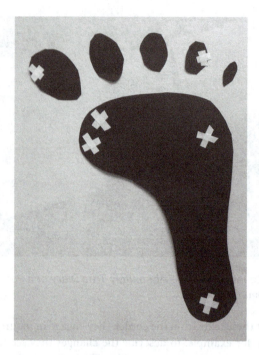

FIGURE 7.2 An icon for poverty: Arnold's blistered foot
Photo: James S. Chisholm.

Additional Resources for Teaching with *The Absolutely True Diary of a Part-Time Indian*

Because of the popularity and power of Alexie's novel, high quality resources abound. There is little more engaging than hearing an author's own voice in relationship to a book—in this case, Alexie's discussion of his life on the NPR interview show, *Fresh Air* (www.npr. org/2017/06/20/533653471/sherman-alexie-says-hes-been-indian-du-jour-for-a-very-long-day) elevates readers' understanding of his writing. His memoir, *You Don't Have to Say You Love Me* (2017), makes connections between Alexie's and Arnold's lives clear.

You may find the curricular materials available in One Book, One Philadelphia (www. freelibrary.org/onebook) especially useful. In addition to that instructional resource, you may want to integrate other texts from Sherman Alexie, such as "Powwow Polaroid" (1998) or his children's book *Thunder Boy Jr.* (2016), illustrated by Yuyi Morales.

To increase your academic understanding of the schooling experiences of American Indian students, we recommend Susan Philips's (1992) and Teresa McCarty's (2002) linguistic and cultural anthropological scholarship, and Joe Suina's (2001) chapter on the impact of traditional schooling in his American Indian community. Contemporary conversations about the schooling and societal experiences of American Indians are taken up in the American Indians in Children's Literature (AICL) blog (https://americanindiansinchildrensliterature.blogspot. com/), which offers resources and recommendations that you may use to choose texts for your classroom. AICL includes critical perspectives specifically on the depiction of indigenous peoples in children's and young adult literature and in society at large (e.g. media, popular culture).

These resources provide compelling background knowledge and personal narratives that contextualize Alexie's novel in ways that highlight additional taboo topics, including the violent excision of cultures and languages of Native peoples in American Indian boarding schools, a schooling context that is echoed by Mr. P., Arnold's mathematics teacher. Mr. P. encourages Arnold to leave the reservation school to attend the all-White high school in Rearden:

> That's how we were taught to teach you. We were supposed to kill the Indian to save the child [...]. We were supposed to make you give up being Indian. Your songs and stories and language and dancing. Everything. We weren't trying to kill Indian people. We were trying to kill Indian culture.
>
> (Alexie, 2007, p. 35)

Visual arts strategies like Cordel and Icons help students approach complex sociocultural and historical contexts in books like *The Absolutely True Diary of a Part-Time Indian*. The Cordel strategy provokes the juxtaposition of different perspectives and modalities to invite students into deeper questions about the historical circumstances and official policies that shape the issues of racism, classism, and alcoholism (among other "isms") that Arnold encounters on the Spokane Indian Reservation and in Rearden. The Icons strategy challenges students to further deepen their meaning making with images as they isolate key concepts from the text to extend their discussions. In short, Cordel and Icons help students to see Arnold and his context in more complex ways, which promotes understanding and empathy—goals that are central to layering literacies through the arts. Next, we explore embodied literacies learning with another contemporary challenging text.

BEING THE TEXT WITH *THE SKIN I'M IN*

Right from the title reference, Sharon Flake's (1998) *The Skin I'm In* calls us to think about embodied literacies. The protagonist, Maleeka, is a smart middle-school student who describes herself as "the darkest, worse-dressed thing in school. I'm also the tallest, skinniest thing you ever seen" (p. 4). Maleeka frames the cruel classmates who pick on her through a description of her own body as she says, "They only see what they see, and they don't seem to like what they see" (p. 5). She introduces us to her mentor teacher Miss Saunders with additional physical descriptions: "She's tall, and fat like nobody's business, and she's got the smallest feet I ever seen. Worse yet, she's got a giant white stain spread halfway across her face like somebody tossed acid on it or something" (p. 1).

For years, Maleeka has endured constant physical and verbal attacks at school and in her neighborhood, particularly because of her dark brown skin. At home, since she was ten, Maleeka has cared for her mom in moments when she can't care for herself due to an overwhelming grief from losing Maleeka's dad in an auto accident. To add to her assaulted image of herself, Maleeka's mom sews her clothes as a seemingly frantic means of surviving her grief. The lopsided and poorly constructed clothes are so embarrassing Maleeka is willing to do the bidding of the meanest girl in school, Char, in exchange for borrowed store-bought clothes. Maleeka completes Char's homework and anything else she demands; in turn, Char brings Maleeka an expensive outfit each morning, which she changes into in the girls' bathroom before first period. The clothes help Maleeka face each school day, but she says, "even those hundred-dollar pants suits she brought in for me to wear can't make up for the hurt I feel when she slaps me with them mean words of hers" (p. 15).

An immediate development in Maleeka's story is Miss Saunders's arrival at her school. Miss Saunders is far from a typical teacher: tall, Black, dressed in business suits from her previous life in corporate America, and with the white "stain" on her face, which she's had from birth. Miss Saunders assigns a lot of reading homework. She challenges the class with discussions about their feelings about how they look and how she looks. She stands up to the students who usually run the school. And she causes disruption with the other teachers due to her "bull in a china shop" ways that resist the curriculum and allegedly push kids too hard. "I'm telling you, hiring her was a bad move," the librarian says to the principal (p. 36). Through Miss Saunders's steady influence, sometimes shocking actions and words, and an assignment to write from the perspective of a 17th-century girl, however, Maleeka discovers that she is a writer. Her imaginary journal for a captured African girl named Akeelma is a source of courage as her perceptions of herself start to change.

Interwoven is the backstory about Maleeka's dad and their relationship. Although Maleeka's mom is incapable of returning to mementos and memories, Maleeka uses traces of her dad to find herself. A small pink mirror he gave her reminds her that he used to say, "I sure could use me a warm cup of cocoa" to tell her he wanted hugs and kisses. Well into the story, Maleeka learns her dad wanted to be a writer and sorts with anticipation through a shoebox of artifacts for a poem her mom says he wrote about her. She finds a crumpled paper bag, on which her dad wrote in careful script about how beautiful, brown, and brilliant his daughter is. With Miss Saunders as a role model, and insights from her father's view of her, throughout the book Maleeka grows to appreciate her body, who she is, and who she wants to be at school.

The Skin I'm In addresses topics that are difficult to read about and discuss in many schools—racism, African American Language (AAL), bullying, and violence—issues that can be controversial and that might cause you and other teachers to want additional background information. Two especially difficult moments in the novel involve physical and emotional violence. In the first instance, two boys on the street assault Maleeka as she's walking home one day. During the attack, they denigrate Maleeka by hurling sexually and racially charged taunts about the skin she's in: "I like a girl with long legs" (p. 92) and "You pretty black thing" (p. 93). In another difficult and pivotal scene, Char threatens to withhold her store-bought clothes from Maleeka and physically assaults her (and threatens to do more) if she does not help Char exact revenge on Miss Saunders. Char's plan involves sneaking into school early in the morning, trashing Miss Saunders's classroom, and setting fire to a pile of foreign currency on Miss Saunders's desk. Although Maleeka hesitates at every turn, Char insists that Maleeka be the one who sets the money on fire and persists: "Char squeezed my shoulder so hard," Maleeka says, "I hear my bones creak" (p. 142). Almost instantaneously the curtains catch fire and the girls run, dropping clothing, article-by-article, as they flee the scene of the fire.

Maleeka's story evokes troubling emotions and raises questions that have no simple answers. Given that many middle school students will connect to the issues Maleeka faces in her daily life, whether their sociocultural contexts or individual identities compare or not, it's necessary to address these issues.

Arts-based Strategies for Being the Text

Many scenes from *The Skin I'm In* offer rich material for arts-based experiences in process drama and movement that encourage students to be the text. Flake's descriptions of characters are visceral and physical, engaging students' imaginations about how to depict Maleeka, Char, and the other adolescents, Miss Saunders and the other faculty, Maleeka's mom, and other characters. Although we still advocate against any kind of simulation activities that would sensationalize or oversimplify the violence Maleeka experiences in her life, Sculpture Garden can be enacted with thoughtfulness. One approach to Sculpture Garden begins with students writing sentences to respond to the question Miss Saunders poses to her class: "What does your face say to the world?" (p. 16). Your students' responses can remain anonymous if you like, or they can write from the perspective of one of the characters rather than themselves. Select several of them (from those whose authors have given permission). For example, Malcolm says, "My face says I'm all that… It says to the homies, I'm the doctor of love. I'm good *to* ya, and good *for* ya" (p. 17). John-John says "his face tells the world he doesn't take no stuff. That people better respect him, or else" (p. 18). Miss Saunders answers the question, as well:

> "My face says I'm smart. Sassy. Sexy. Self-confident," she says, snapping her fingers rapid-fire. "It says I'm caring and, yes, even a little cold sometimes. See these laugh lines," she says, almost poking herself in the eyes. "They let people know that I love a good joke. These tiny bags? They tell the world I like to stay up late." … "What do I think my face says to the world? I think it says I'm all that," she says, snapping her fingers.
>
> (p. 20)

Read selected sentences aloud as pairs of students sculpt one another into physicalized expressions of what the responses mean. As each set of sculptors finishes their work, invite the audience of peers to notice details, comment, reflect, and ask questions before taking their own turn as sculptors and clay.

Dramatic Performances that become Staged Performances offer the means for students to share their insights from *The Skin I'm In* with a broader audience of peers and/or family and community members, and create authentic purposes for students to seek out additional texts and connections to deepen understanding. The Additional Resources section that follows suggests body image and AAL as two specific directions for further study, and your students will contribute other productive ideas. In Staged Performances related to *The Diary of a Young Girl*, students connect historical injustices during the Holocaust to contemporary issues like domestic violence and eating disorders. In response to Maleeka's story, students might revise and rehearse the results of Sculpture Garden and other process drama experiences like Tableau or Pantomime, or they might write new monologues or perform scenes or monologues written by others (peers or published). Staged Performances needn't become costly or laborious productions in terms of costumes or sets; in fact, they may have stronger effect if they are produced simply with all performers dressed in black and black boxes on stage for chairs or other props. The point is to engage students by learning about the themes of the book through and in their bodies. Many of these embodied moments can occur in the regular course of the day and week, in the classroom, and without significant preparation. The presence of an audience, whether spontaneous or formal is key.

Additional Resources for Teaching with *The Skin I'm In*

Several themes in *The Skin I'm In* suggest directions for additional materials and areas of study. Most evident, from the first pages, is racial identity. Maleeka experiences colorism, or skin color prejudice, throughout the novel. Considered by many to be a controversial topic, Black-on-Black discrimination is an effect of plantation politics—"a fabric interwoven within the Black society as a result of slavery" (Busey, 2014, p. 128)—that persists today. Christopher Busey suggests critical literacy and arts-based instructional activities that focus on media, including analyzing photographs for viewers' biases about attractiveness and intelligence, and critically analyzing and discussing popular films and television shows. The curriculum he describes emphasizes contemporary evidence of centuries-old discriminatory practices.

The topics of body image and definitions of beauty, within and outside of the African American community, are important and of interest to middle grade and adolescent readers. There are numerous references to mirrors in *The Skin I'm In*. Maleeka finds a small mirror her father gave her as a little girl that gives her strength. The mirrors in the girls' bathroom at school are sources of courage and of trouble. The lyrics of Sweet Honey in the Rock's song, "No Mirrors in My Nana's House," and the picturebook by the same title (Barnwell, 1998) suggest that beauty and self-concepts are reflected in the eyes of those who love us. The illustrations are minimalist paintings by Synthia Saint James, the lyrics are poetry, and the vocals are a cappella, inviting students into movement and dance responses, and additional poetry writing.

The Dove campaign, including videos and materials available at www.dove.com/us/en/stories/campaigns.html, is designed to expand and challenge conventional definitions of beauty, including hashtag campaigns like #womengettold and #beautybias. Curriculum materials for teachers of 11–14-year-olds are available at http://selfesteem.dove.us/Articles/Written/Teachers-and-schools.aspx. These materials are excellent for supporting students' creations for Staged Performances.

AAL is another theme for exploration in *The Skin I'm In*. Maleeka tells her story in first person, and she and her classmates speak AAL consistently. Miss Saunders and the other adults, on the other hand, speak White Vernacular English. Although never addressed directly within the book, the presence of AAL is an invitation to study how power is inherent in language variation in schools and communities. PBS offers an excellent set of classroom resources called, "Do You Speak American," with a section devoted to AAL (www.pbs.org/speak/seatosea/americanvarieties/AAVE/). An Ebonics timeline, for example, provides background knowledge for teachers and ignites questions for students' inquiries. Vershawn Ashanti Young (2014) explains, argues for, and offers teaching strategies about code-meshing, or "merging language variations," as opposed to code-switching, "separating languages according to context" (p. 1). We encourage you to engage students in inquiries about the local language(s) and language variations of their communities and neighborhoods, and the power inherent in the ways they are sanctioned, exploited, and policed, especially at school. Results from such studies can be shared with classmates and families as dramatic performances, videos, public service announcements, and so on.

Sculpture Garden and Dramatic and Staged Performances are valuable ways to engage students in challenging texts like *The Skin I'm In* because they get students out of their seats to learn in and through their bodies. In these instructional strategies students deliberately use their bodies to make sense of the text; their bodies then become texts to be read by others. Like several of the teachers you've met in this book, if you are new to process drama activities you might feel apprehensive about taking risks with being the text. Frequent community-building strategies throughout a study help teachers and students feel safe enough to take such risks. The power of layering is also significant here, as being the text is even more effective when layered with seeing and feeling the text.

FEELING THE TEXT WITH *ENRIQUE'S JOURNEY: THE TRUE STORY OF A BOY DETERMINED TO REUNITE WITH HIS MOTHER (ADAPTED FOR YOUNG PEOPLE)*

In *Enrique's Journey* (2013), Pulitzer Prize award-winning author, Sonia Nazario, presents a stirring portrait of a young boy, Enrique, as he grows up in Honduras without his mother, Lourdes, who leaves Enrique and his sister, Belky, to provide for them by earning money in the United States. Nazario documents Enrique's confusion, hope, sorrow, and anger as he tries to understand why his mother never returns. With journalistic precision, Nazario pivots between the challenges Enrique faces in Honduras and the struggles and disappointment Lourdes faces first in California, and then in North Carolina as an undocumented immigrant. For example, Enrique moves from living with his father who begins a new family separate from Enrique and his sister, to living with his grandmother, María, with whom he "share[s] a tiny shack, thirty feet square, in Carrizal, one of Tegucigalpa's [the capital of Honduras] poorest neighborhoods. Grandmother María built it herself with wooden slats. Enrique can see daylight through the cracks" (Nazario, 2013, p. 25). Enrique's relationship with his grandmother María becomes too much for her to endure when he begins to act out in school, gets suspended, stays out too late on the street, and hangs with "bad" boys. Grandmother María writes to Lourdes to tell her that Enrique must find a new home. "To Enrique, it is another rejection. First his mother, then his father, and now his grandmother María" (p. 38).

Just when it seems like Enrique might find some stable footing living with his loving Uncle Marco, tragedy strikes again when Enrique's Uncle Marco and Uncle Victor are killed in a currency exchange operation gone bad. This event has profound consequences for Enrique both physically and emotionally. For Lourdes, too, the deaths of her brothers are almost too much to bear. Lourdes pays for the funerals, which depletes entirely the seven hundred dollars she had saved over nine years to pay a "coyote" or smuggler to bring her children into the United States.

Enrique's uncles' deaths send him into an emotional tailspin. He sinks deeper into a drug addiction that disrupts his relationship in his new home with his grandmother Águeda, where seven other people already live: "besides Grandmother Águeda, there are two aunts and four young cousins. They are poor. Nonetheless, Grandmother Águeda takes Enrique in" (p. 41). Despite Lourdes's financial support and the material possessions she provides for her children, they long to be with her and would exchange everything just to have their mother with them.

While living at Grandmother Águeda's, Enrique, 15, falls in love with María Isabel, "the girl next door" (p. 41), who becomes the only consistent support system for Enrique. He begins to steal from his aunts to pay his drug dealers who threaten to kill him if he doesn't. Enrique ultimately realizes that he will either end up on the streets or die if he stays in Tegucigalpa. He decides to leave to find his mother. Despite María Isabel's pleas for him to stay—especially since she may be pregnant—Enrique embarks on his journey with astonishingly few resources.

Enrique's journey exposes the dangerous 1,564-mile route from Tegucigalpa to Nuevo Laredo, Mexico, where migrants camp and work and wait for smugglers to help them cross the river into the United States. Part II of *Enrique's Journey* portrays, with brutal detail, the hardship Enrique endures as he attempts this journey eight times. On tops of trains, Enrique moves northbound from his Central American country through Guatemala and Chiapas, in southern Mexico, and learns about *la migra*—Mexican immigration officers who escort Enrique to the "Bus of Tears" back to Guatemala. Enrique learns about the stops along the way where *la migra* are likely to be. He also encounters corrupt police officers, bandits, gangsters, thieves, rapists, and murderers, as well as compassionate people who, although they have very little to give Enrique to support him on his way, give all that they can nonetheless.

Despite witnessing countless rapes, beatings, and deaths of migrants traveling on tops of trains and despite falling asleep and being brutally attacked himself, Enrique persists, determined to find his mother in the United States. In one particularly violent assault, three men jump Enrique on the train, take everything but his underwear, viciously beat him after they learn that he has only fifty pesos on his person, and break his teeth, which "rattle like broken glass in his mouth" (p. 59). They contemplate throwing Enrique off the train, but he begs for his life, escapes momentarily from them and jumps off the train himself to avoid their gunfire. It is so dark, Enrique can't see the blood, but he can feel the warmth of it spreading over his body, which throbs as a result of the brutalization he experienced on the train.

Ultimately, and notwithstanding monumental obstacles every step of the way, Enrique is smuggled into the United States and is reunited with his mother, who is living with her daughter, Diana, and Lourdes's boyfriend. After a brief period of relief and joy from being together again, Enrique's feelings slowly, then fiercely emerge, regarding his mother's decision to leave him and his sister when he was only five years old. Lourdes, whose separation from Enrique and Belky has tortured her, convinces herself that her sacrifices were in the best interest of her children. Although Enrique stopped going to school after suspension and being held back, his sister Belky excelled and attended schools that Lourdes paid for. Lourdes has also struggled to make ends meet and save money to send back home to her family. High rental rates, immigration raids, and gang violence compel Lourdes to second guess her most consequential decision to leave her family behind.

Throughout all of these experiences, readers feel how for Enrique and Lourdes, every step forward in developing their relationship is followed by two steps backward. Readers are thrust into an emotional landscape in which every attempt to improve one's station in life is met with an obstacle to overcome. Importantly, this portrait provides a human story and an immigration counter narrative for circulation in society. Perhaps now more than ever, feeling this text can be a call to action for comprehensive immigration reform in the United States, where the current approach to stem the flow of migrants seems to add only additional physical and policy barriers.

Enrique's Journey is a challenging text for many reasons. First, the topic of immigration is politically charged, to which parents, teachers, and students may object (Hess & McAvoy, 2015). The fact that Enrique is not a literary character, but an actual human being—of whom photographs in the book "prove" his existence—only further complicates the potentially political reception of this text in schools. In light of the current U.S. President's immigration ban and intention to build a wall on the U.S./Mexico border, it is difficult to imagine how Enrique's story can be told without also discussing current immigration policies and larger nationalist, populist stances toward immigration across the globe where refugee crises indicate that civil and deliberative discourse is needed, but not often realized.

Second, *Enrique's Journey* includes unsanctioned school topics including but not limited to rape, teenage pregnancy, drug abuse, and non-sexual violence. And third, Enrique's sociocultural circumstances may be unfamiliar to many teachers: the Spanish language, the country of Honduras, Central American customs, and the realities of immigration stories to the United States. Although clearly challenging per our own definition, we believe in the power of *Enrique's Journey* as a text with the potential to promote civil discourse, and to elevate students' inquiries into difficult topics that matter.

Arts-based Strategies for Feeling the Text

> Children like Enrique dream that when they finally find their mothers, they will live happily ever after. For weeks—months, even—the mothers and children hold on to a fairy-tale idea of how they should feel toward one another. Then their true feelings surface.
>
> (p. 163)

Many readers of *Enrique's Journey* may not realize that thousands of mothers leave their children in their home countries and enter the United States unlawfully in order to support their children. Nazario stumbled upon this realization when she innocently asked her housekeeper, Carmen, if she planned to have any more children than the one she was raising. Carmen's emotional response to Nazario revealed that she did, indeed, have four other children, whom she had not seen for 12 years as she worked in the United States to support them. Carmen recounts a heartbreaking story that convinced her to make the most difficult decision of her life and leave her children in order to seek opportunity:

> "They would ask me for food, and I didn't have it." Many nights, they went to bed without dinner. She tried to quiet their hunger pangs as she lulled them to sleep. "Sleep face-down so your stomach won't growl so much," Carmen would say, gently coaxing them to turn over.
>
> (p. 2)

Not unlike the experiences of Holocaust survivors and their descendants, many readers can't imagine circumstances such as Carmen's. And certainly, we imagine, people don't have Carmen's story in mind when they chant "Build that Wall!" at political rallies or use such sayings to ostracize immigrants in their communities. Boyd and Dyches (2017) argue that teachers can develop their students' "critical awareness" of immigration "in order to develop their empathy and social consciousness" (p. 33). *Enrique's Journey* challenges readers to feel the text—to inhabit the perspectives of the people Nazario writes about and to construct, in response, a counter narrative about immigration.

To prepare students for the emotions that Enrique's story provokes, we recommend Creating Thick Air. Fred Gross's and Michael Schubert's stories about survival during the Holocaust contextualize eighth-graders' reading of Anne Frank's diary. Similarly, you can invite people who have migrated to the United States to share their stories with your students, which will personalize and make relevant what is otherwise an extraordinary story, far removed from the lives of most middle grades students. Creating Thick Air bonds storytellers with their audiences. Indeed, too many middle grades students have dangerous migration stories as a part of their personal and family life narratives. It's important to provide students with the space in which to tell those stories—not only to support their learning of a new language and to build their identities at school, but to teach non-immigrants about the rest of the world. Middle grades students who have never had to move anywhere for any reason, will feel the text as well, by hearing about how immigrants sustained or lost relationships, how they endured hardships along the way, or how they adjusted to an entirely new place to call home, devoid of familiar ways of life that some students might take for granted. Inviting members of a school community to tell their immigration stories personalizes a political topic in ways that can potentially change the narrative. We talk about issues differently when we put real faces to abstract topics.

Immigration stories mobilize emotion from the community into the classroom. In turn, Marquee can move emotional literacies from the classroom into the community. Pulling excerpts that prompt readers to inhabit newcomers' perspectives and feelings that they might never have considered before can open spaces for conversations around immigration policies, stances, reform, and resources. Imagine reading on your school's marquee the following:

> "They would ask me for food, and I didn't have it… Sleep facedown so your stomach won't growl so much."
>
> —María del Carmen Ferrez, Mother, Emigrated 1985 from Guatemala.

Not all immigration stories prompt heartbreaking feelings, and a wide selection shows students there is no one single immigration story. The website myimmigrationstory.com is a digital space for U.S. immigrants to tell their stories "in their own words," and provides teachers with firsthand accounts if they're not locally available. It's easy to select from the website stories specifically written by adolescents with whom your students can connect to Anne, Enrique, and themselves. Excerpts of the following stories on a marquee invite the community into dialogue and deeper reflection about the complexities of immigration in the United States:

> "We couldn't go back [to Yemen] so we decided to stay."
>
> —Basam, New York

> "I don't know anything about Mexico because I was raised here and I find myself scared to be deported to a place that I do not know."
>
> —Gonzalo, Florida

> "I've been illegal all my life but found out when I was 15."
>
> —Jose, Florida

> "I have been apart from my wife and kids for 4 years now… Maybe it is because my name is Mohamed & I am Muslim. If that's the problem I am ready to change my name & religion if that will help me to see my family."
>
> —Mohamed, Tunisia

> "It is my main goal to finish college and look [at] my mom and thank her for staying and making my dreams come true of being someone in life."
>
> —Anonymous, California

> "You know sometimes it can get hard not having papers… I'm 13 and this immigration stuff gets to me every day. I just want to go back home with my real family."
>
> —Guadalupe, Michigan

> "I have done all I can the legal way to obtain a green card but I feel like the system has failed me. I have lived in a prison for 25 years and I have committed no crime."
>
> —Denise, USA

> "My dad was deported when I was 16 years old. I know he is somewhere in the Dominican Republic, if he is still alive."
>
> —Emilia, Massachusetts

Additional Resources for Teaching with *Enrique's Journey*

In addition to myimmigrationstory.com, Sonia Nazario's website, enriquesjourney.com, features resources like articles she's written in the *New York Times*, a TEDx talk she gave in Washington DC, and specific materials that teachers and students can use in the classroom. The instructor's materials section on Nazario's website links to numerous lesson plans and approaches to teaching *Enrique's Journey* in middle school, high school, and college classrooms. You'll find there excerpts from her keynote speech for teachers on the Power of Stories at the 2014 National Council of Teachers of English conference, multimodal videos made for and by students (e.g. an Emmy award-winning movie trailer/Public Service Announcement for *Enrique's Journey* made by San Diego high school students, a documentary film, a PowerPoint presentation), inspiring and beautiful student artwork, and Spanish language resources.

One student-made movie trailer for *Enrique's Journey* features a book club discussion with San Diego high school students. One young woman says, "I would recommend this book to students because, to me, this story made me feel like I was in Enrique's shoes. And I could feel what he felt going through." This student continues, "The way Sonia describes those scenes, it's exciting, because it makes you feel like you're there." We can't imagine a more powerful testament to the importance of feeling a text than the conversation represented in this book club discussion. Students link their feelings to their engagement with the narrative and Enrique's life, and ultimately reflect on how much they have to appreciate in their own lives, including the sacrifices that their families have made for them.

THE EVOLVING NATURE OF CHALLENGING TEXTS

In this chapter, we extend what we have learned about the power of layering literacies in teaching and learning about *The Diary of a Young Girl* into thinking about three additional challenging texts with contemporary content. Layering *seeing*, *being*, and *feeling the text* through the arts engages learners physically, cognitively, and emotionally in deep reading and empathetic responses as they confront texts that demand all of our attentions.

We consider challenging those texts that present unsanctioned or taboo topics, about which teachers feel underprepared, and which evoke emotions that are troubling. Although *The Diary*, our exemplar challenging text, is historically situated, it's important to realize that the nature of texts as challenging isn't going away. How topics are deemed "challenging" changes over time. For a long period of time, for example, texts and topics that included lesbian, gay, bisexual, and transgender (LGBT) themes were considered extremely challenging and literature with LGBT characters was regularly banned. This literature is now, happily, much more commonplace. As the sociocultural climate evolves, and particular literature is situated within it, we continue to need tools to approach whatever texts and topics are currently challenging, and methods for inviting students into conversations about them. We realize that all three of the texts reviewed in this chapter may not be challenging texts in your community. We invite you, though, to consider the local social justice issues to which you are committed as a teacher and to which your students are committed. We invite you to select texts that speak powerfully to those issues, and to leverage the arts to support students in grappling with the complexities inherent in them that deserve our collective risk-taking.

The students you've met in this book take risks with seeing, being, and feeling the text as related to the Holocaust. In Chapter 8, we consider how and why as students complete the Visual

Learning Analysis that teaches us about their arts-based learning. We build on their insights to theorize how they approach such a challenging and difficult topic with respect. We argue that adolescents desire to work with historical and contemporary challenging texts and topics and predict that your students will exceed expectations for treating challenging texts with respect in your context as well.

REFERENCES

Abramovitch, I. (2012). Teaching Anne Frank in the United States. In B. Kirshenblatt-Gimblett & J. Shandler (Eds.), *Anne Frank unbound: Media, imagination, memory.* Bloomington: Indiana University Press.

Alexie, S. (1998). Powwow polaroid. In D. Haynes & J. Landsman (Eds.), *Welcome to your life: Writings for the heart of young America.* Minneapolis, MN: Milkweed Additions.

Alexie, S. (2007). *The absolutely true diary of a part-time Indian.* Illus. E. Forney. New York, NY: Little, Brown and Company.

Alexie, S. (2016). *Thunder Boy Jr.* Illus. Y. Morales. New York, NY: Little, Brown and Company.

Alexie, S. (2017). *You don't have to say you love me: A memoir.* New York, NY: Little, Brown and Company.

Barnwell, Y. M. (1998). *No mirrors in my nana's house.* Illus. S. S. James. Boston, MA: Houghton Mifflin Harcourt.

Boyd, A., & Dyches, J. (2017). Taking down walls: Countering dominant narratives of the immigrant experience through the teaching of *Enrique's journey. The ALAN Review, 44*(2), 31–42.

Britzman, D. (1998). *Lost subject, contested objects: Toward a psychoanalytic inquiry of learning.* New York, NY: SUNY Press.

Buehler, J. (2016). *Teaching reading with YA literature: Complex texts, complex lives.* Urbana, IL: National Council of Teachers of English.

Busey, C. L. (2014). Examining race from within: Black intraracial discrimination in social studies curriculum. *Social Studies Research & Practice, 9*(2), 120–131.

Crandall, B. R. (2009). Adding a disability perspective when reading adolescent literature: Sherman Alexie's *The absolutely true diary of a part-time Indian. The ALAN Review, 36*(2), 71–78.

Flake, S. (1998). *The skin I'm in.* New York, NY: Hyperion Books.

Frank, A. (1952). *The diary of a young girl.* New York, NY: Bantam.

Hess, D. E., & McAvoy, P. (2015). *The political classroom: Evidence and ethics in democratic education.* New York, NY: Routledge.

McCarty, T. L. (2002). *A place to be Navajo: Rough Rock and the struggle for self-determination in indigenous schooling.* New York, NY: Routledge.

Nazario, S. (2013). *Enrique's journey: The true story of a boy determined to reunite with his mother (Adapted for young people).* New York, NY: Random House.

O'Donnell-Allen, C. (2011). *Tough talk, tough texts: Teaching English to change the world.* Portsmouth, NH: Heinemann.

Philips, S. U. (1992). *The invisible culture: Communication in classroom and community on the Warm Springs Indian Reservation.* Prospect Heights, IL: Waveland Press.

Suina, J. (2001). And then I went to school: Memories of a Pueblo childhood. In A. G. Meléndez, M. J. Young, P. Moore, & P. Pynes (Eds.), *The multicultural Southwest: A reader* (pp. 91–96). Tucson: University of Arizona Press.

Talbert, K. (2012). Using *The absolutely true diary of a part-time Indian* to teach about racial formation. *Journal of Curriculum Theorizing, 28*(1), 266–271.

Young, V. A. (2014). Introduction: Are you part of the conversation? In V. A. Young, R. Barrett, Y. Y. Rivera, & K. B. Lovejoy (Eds.), *Other people's English: Code-meshing, code-switching, and African American literacy* (pp. 1–11). New York, NY: Teachers College Press.

Chapter 8
Standing Next to Anne Frank
Layering Literacies and Challenging Topics with Respect

Our goal in this book is to examine ways in which arts-based literacy engagements enhance students' visual, embodied, and emotional transactions with challenging texts and topics. We call this layering literacies through the arts. As Jeff Jamner suggests in the Foreword, although we are convinced by our work in the Anne Frank: Bearing Witness Project that arts-based literacy engagements *do* accomplish important outcomes for learners and teachers, we are more invested in understanding *why* and *how*. Therefore, in this chapter, we reflect on *why* it matters for students to be able to read Anne Frank's diary in powerful ways that promote their learning and empathetic response. We further explore *how* it happens by considering students' respect for the topic, which emerges as an important theme in students' responses to their study of *The Diary of a Young Girl*. Ultimately, we see how topic, community, and characters help students to "stand next to Anne Frank" and generate respect for the Holocaust.

APPROACHING THE HOLOCAUST WITH RESPECT

The theme of respect emerges in robust ways as students participate in the process of Visual Learning Analysis (VLA), in which they examine and discuss photos of their arts-based learning. In the VLA process, students explain how they connect aspects of each photo with issues of embodied and emotional meaning making, risk-taking, movement, and empathy. We recognize in the VLA a productive means for documenting the social-emotional, affective learning that occurs in arts-based study of challenging texts and topics. Throughout the study, students' written reflections and classroom discussions confirm the value of respect for the topic in their learning. In the next sections, we illustrate how the topics students address, the community in which students encounter them, and the historical and fictional characters they meet in literature matter.

The Topic Matters

As students discuss how gaze, gesture, posture, and proximity are evident in photographs of arts-based learning in their classrooms, they regularly mention how "serious," "sensitive," and "important" the topic is and recognize the Holocaust as a "tragic" human event. Although it may not be surprising to connect these terms with a study of the Holocaust, students frame these characteristics as consequential to their meaning making.

For example, in Kim Joiner's classroom, Lauren writes on her VLA, "As you can see from the picture, everyone was being very quiet. This is because this is a very powerful subject and I

In this picture all the people seem to be focusing on the pictures, they're all sort of close together really seeming to work together. All the expressions on there faces are either curious or focused as well, like they're really thinking things out. Pat seems to be looking over at Tom which makes me think he was probably talking to the group about the pictures, which could be risky on his part due to some of the pictures being graphic and really depressing and even just shocking to look at especially to descuss. You can definitely see, like I said before, just the seriousness, the focus, and even just the shock of realizing that these pictures were something that actually happened.

FIGURE 8.1 Evan's Visual Learning Analysis (VLA) illustrates how the topic matters
Photo: James S. Chisholm.

think it is better to understand something if you are quiet and are thinking to yourself." Lauren's comments respond to the same image featured in Figure 2.8, in which students examine Holocaust texts on the cordel. Lauren reads "quiet" in student posture, proximity, and gaze. And she connects this quiet with the power of the subject matter. "It's a serious topic, and everyone seems to understand that and [they] aren't goofing off," Lillian writes on her VLA based on a close-up image of her classmates as they read texts on the cordel. And one of Kelly Holland's students, Isabel, writes on her VLA that

> Most people were quiet during this time because they were looking at the pictures of what happened to the people during the Holocaust. Those pictures helped out a lot because reality "smacks you in the face" and actually proves to you how bad the Holocaust was. This activity was risky but sometimes we need to do risky things to learn and understand things better.

Isabel's response illustrates the collective respect for the topic she and her classmates demonstrate, which emerges from her visual analysis of embodied meanings in a classroom photo. Isabel also reiterates the power of the visual image as it has a physical and emotional effect on her—"it smacks you in the face."

In Kelly's classroom, a small group of students gathers around a table to examine photographs from *My Secret Camera: Life in the Łódź Ghetto* (Smith & Grossman, 2008) to build a chronology of events from the Holocaust. Evan selects a photo of the chronology activity for the VLA (see Figure 8.1). He identifies the "graphic," "depressing," and "shocking" nature of the photographs his classmates examine, but he also comments on the effect of the images on his classmates' embodied responses: "You can definitely see, like I said before, just the seriousness, the focus, and even just the shock of realizing that these pictures were something that actually happened." Evan's commentary conveys well how students' bodies and emotions reveal their respect for the topic.

The Classroom Community Matters

Although never prompted, students often use words that convey the idea of community to describe the arts-based activities, and emphasize their proximity to one another as an indicator of community. Comments like "I felt a sense of community. Everybody is like, together, reading about a serious topic" and frequent mention of "togetherness" indicate their sense that the topic is best approached as a group to increase understanding and interpersonal comfort. Some students write that they see themselves as "mature" and able to cope with the atrocities they are studying. As one student reflects at the end of the study, "I think this unit made me more mature and allowed me to see the beauty in some of Anne Frank's quotes." In their reflections, students often use the pronoun "we" which emphasizes the group, and yet, students sometimes qualify their points about being in a group by suggesting that even within a community their experiences are singular and personal.

For her VLA, Lizzy selects a photograph of two of her classmates, Dawn and Brooke, during a Dramatic Performance in Kim's classroom (see Figure 8.2). The performance dramatizes Anne's diary entry from March 25, 1943, when she describes a suspected burglary of her father's warehouse within which the secret annex existed. Anne writes about the emotional turmoil this

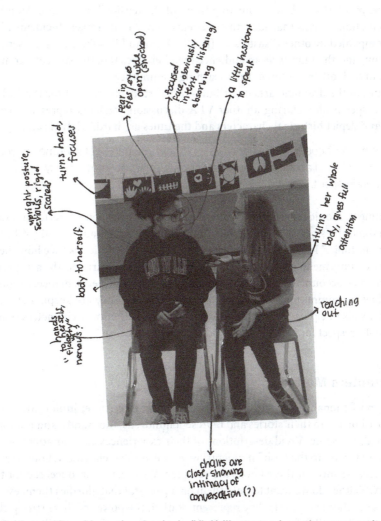

FIGURE 8.2 Lizzy's Visual Learning Analysis (VLA) illustrates how the community matters
Photo: James S. Chisholm.

event caused for her: "[Margot] was trying to calm me down since I'd turned white as chalk and was extremely nervous" (Frank, 1952, pp. 89–90). Dawn and Brooke convey this emotion well with their bodies as the passage is narrated by another student outside of the frame.

Lizzy's VLA response evidences how successful Dawn and Brooke are in conveying the emotions Anne wrote about in this entry. But Lizzy's writing also reflects the ways in which her classmates' bodies convey the strength of their learning community. For instance, Lizzy draws an arrow on the photo between Dawn and Brooke and writes, "Chairs are close, showing intimacy of conversation." Lizzy circles Brooke's back and notes how she "turns her whole body, [and] gives full attention." About Dawn's gaze, Lizzy notes her "focused face, obviously intent on listening/absorbing," and draws a circle around Dawn's head. Lizzy's words reflect her strong classroom community as Dawn and Brooke work through the meanings of the diary passage. The emotions associated with being violated during a robbery and not knowing if or when such a violation would occur again are familiar to many. The entry emphasizes Anne's physical response: "everyone's stomach was churning from all the tension" (p. 91) and Anne's words describe the emotional stress that such an experience leaves in its wake: "Incidents like these are always accompanied by other disasters…" (p. 91). Dawn and Brooke, as actors, sense this emotional tension, and then Lizzy, as an audience member, does too; the students' commitment to the scene and each other reinforces their learning community.

The nature of the dramatic arts contributes to the students' respect for the Holocaust, and Anne Frank specifically. During another VLA discussion, students represent their efforts to dramatize and depict historical characters and the times as "hard." Calvin says,

> I think it's harder because it's a sensitive topic and you can't get it wrong, so you [worry] how do I do this so I accurately represent it and don't, you know, in any way poke fun at it? Don't undersize it. Don't make it less than it actually is.

To this comment, Monica says, "That's what I'm afraid of, that when we perform is that we don't fully understand the story so then it looks funny, but we don't want to make it funny because this is a serious topic." In this exchange between Calvin and Monica, we see how the arts mediate students' commitment to the topic and their community of learners. The arts prompt Calvin and Monica to be accountable to the disciplinary standards for performance, to their audience to whom they are communicating, and to Anne's story that they are keeping alive. These and other students also help us understand how historical and fictional characters matter as they shape students' respect for challenging topics like the Holocaust.

The Characters Matter

Historical and fictional characters in challenging texts, like Anne, Junior, Maleeka, and Enrique, endure horrors in their stories and represent hundreds, thousands, and millions of others who endure(d) the same. Vivid descriptions of their experiences call our attention and engage us. They cause for us "in the flesh" moments, when we are shaken. And yet our relationships to the adolescents we meet in these books are complex. We don't want to feel sad for them in the sense of pity. Neither do we want to hold them on a pedestal that glorifies them, especially over the millions of other real people they represent. Rather, the power of these strong characters is that they make it possible for us to enter challenging and complex topics through "one"—they are access points to, and humanize, the difficult topics beyond distanced statistics.

Student Voice Box

I saw a video of Anne taken at a wedding, with her head out of her house window. I could see that she was just like me, a young girl fascinated by the people getting married on the street.

Liam, eighth-grade student

The students describe their learning about Anne Frank's diary with phrases such as "stepping into the shoes [of Anne]," "she's our friend," "she was so close to us," and "we've like taken them in." Consider how Lillian expresses her relationship to Anne as her body becomes the annex during Pantomime,

> I wanted to be a part of her life. Like the house was a big thing and how she was in a very small space. Like a table to write the diary on. And then her thoughts, Monica was like her thoughts, like acting it out. So everybody had a part of Anne Frank's life.

These are empathetic expressions. Students also connect, as many readers do, to Anne's station in life—her complicated relationship with her mother, sibling rivalry, having a crush, and everyday annoyances.

Student Voice Box

I felt really connected when she really expressed how angry she was and when we got into a circle and talked about how things in this book can and are happening in our lives.

Danielle, eighth-grade student

Eighth-grade students teach us, through their bodies, their words, and their thoughts, that by the end of their study of the Holocaust they feel connected to Anne. We theorize these connections as "standing next to" a character and we suggest that standing next to a character might be a position all readers can take when dealing with challenging texts. In fact, standing next to a strong, heroic character might embolden us to take risks as readers and learners, and eventually, to take actions that matter. We argue that creating arts-based learning opportunities for students to "stand next to" Anne, Junior, Maleeka, and Enrique, and other strong figures from challenging literature, is part of developing respect for challenging topics. Students help us see how and why important topics, strong communities of learners, and compelling historical and fictional characters all matter. They are essential to the process of layering literacies through the arts to support students' respect for the Holocaust and topics encountered in other challenging texts.

STANDING NEXT TO ADOLESCENTS

Studying difficult topics, building strong classroom communities, and inviting students to stand next to historical and fictional characters mediate adolescents' respect for the content they encounter in challenging texts. We suggest layering literacies through the arts as a means toward this end. Through the stories we tell in this book, we demonstrate that adolescents are interested in studying serious and difficult topics, and when in supportive classroom contexts, they are fully able to engage deeply with challenging texts. Therefore, we resist deficit perspectives about adolescents and adolescence that may circulate in schools and communities—assumptions that restrict learners' opportunities to experience emotional and embodied learning.

As we describe in Chapter 1, some educators and parents think about challenging topics and young learners through the lens of a discourse of innocence, in which, although well-intentioned, adults seek to shield children and young people from truths about atrocities in the world. Similarly, widespread and erroneous discourses about adolescence can prevent teachers and students from building the trust necessary for taking risks with difficult topics. We argue that layering literacies through the arts can support our collective rejection of discourses that characterize adolescents as disinterested, apathetic, plugged in, distracted, egocentric, and driven by their hormones (among other stereotypes that circulate in society). Since reading challenging texts is a relational literacy practice that depends on the quality of the classroom community co-constructed by teachers and students, we encourage you to reflect about, and if necessary, rethink perspectives that limit opportunities and lower expectations for adolescents.

Listen to Oscar's thoughts about ways in which he and his classmates are already living out some of the lessons of *The Diary*:

> It's been over 70 years since the end of the war and the survivors have had kids and they have had kids. We are those grandchildren and great grandchildren to some survivors. And I believe we already have empathy. All these kids [in a photo of his classmates] are communicating and there are different races and realms of life.

Oscar, like so many other students, reminds us of the potential for our own learning as educators when we create spaces in the classroom for students to voice their understandings. Indeed, he also challenges us to recognize and build upon the empathy that students have already cultivated in their own lives.

Listen also to Liam, who reflects on his study of *The Diary* and the meanings he is taking from that experience:

> I also think it's kind of like, it scars you. Kind of like a useful scar. So what I mean by useful scar is like, yeah, it hurts in the process of getting it, but afterwards … like in the context of the Holocaust and being aware, it scars you to be aware, but it scars you in a way that you're never going to do it again. It's a lesson you learn and it teaches you how to be aware and allow it not to happen because once you hurt yourself and get a scar, you know, 'Oh, I'm not going to do that again.' You know? So if you're dicing something and you cut your finger, I'm not going to cut my finger next time.

As we read and reread Liam's expression of such an elegant metaphor for *The Diary of a Young Girl*, we recognize it as a useful way to think about layering literacies. A scar is visual, embodied, and emotional. The visual evidence of a scar, its inscription on the body, and its message to feel and to relate to others reflect how meaningful deep learning experiences are. Scars, like deep learning, make it impossible to forget—we can see scars, touch scars, and feel scars. Scars connect people to their pasts and can shape their identities, as well as how they might live out their present lives. Even if others can't identify the scar, its owner knows that it's there. Michael Schubert's mom had the tattooed numbers on her arm removed as soon as she could when she was 19. There is a scar—a "patch of shiny skin"—that remains.

Oscar and Liam show us the power of challenging texts to promote lasting reminders of the lessons that are still being learned, in this case, from the Holocaust. Reminiscent of the ways in which some Holocaust survivors perceive their tattooed numbers from the concentration camps, the visual imprints itself on our minds and bodies in ways that demand our attention and sensemaking.

Teacher Voice Box

What are our central obligations as educators? We have to honor the history of the Holocaust as a sacred place. We also have to honor and preserve the six million. We are going into their deaths. We are harvesting from their suffering lessons, ideas, ways to challenge and open the eyes and the hearts of students. There has to be an obligation to the Jewish victims of the Holocaust and what is that? We're also obligated to remember that we're taking a risk. We are gathering our students around one of the most gruesome times in history. We are gathering them around an abyss, a great darkness. We are the boundary between becoming lost and becoming informed. We have to remember there is an obligation to their emotional safety, physical safety, and spiritual safety. We really want our students to be left with memories; to be given hope in spite of the darkness, to be made wise and not cynical, to be called into compassion and not into indifference.

Fred Whittaker, science and religion teacher

We acknowledge that teaching about Anne Frank and the Holocaust is challenging for all of the ways we've explored in this book—there are taboo or unsanctioned topics inherent in studying the Holocaust, the subject matter demands deep and broad knowledge across a number of disciplines, and the individual and collective stories can be emotionally overwhelming. We also acknowledge that some students in the Anne Frank: Bearing Witness Project did not connect with Anne and responded to their study in ways that either sanctified or trivialized Anne Frank's life and the Holocaust—two risks that Schweber (2006) encountered in her own college-level course on the Holocaust. Nevertheless, each chapter in this book offers ambitious arts-based approaches for reading challenging texts and learning about challenging topics that we hope not only lead to more powerful teaching and learning opportunities for teachers and students alike, but also support an education agenda that promotes students' empathy and critical consciousness.

MORE QUESTIONS THAN ANSWERS

We close by returning to our personal experiences with this study. It had been decades since either of us had read *The Diary*. Our study of adolescents and teachers learning about *The Diary* became a true inquiry for us. We hoped we could learn from the students, their teachers, and the arts educators about what "embodied learning" means, and why we should continue to advocate for the arts as a meaningful part of significant learning. As we learned "in the field" at four very different school sites, we turned to the literature to help us understand the data. We aren't artists, but since this study began we've steadily learned about the arts, taking part in professional development sessions about drama, increasing our knowledge about photography and other visual arts, and reading extensively about arts-based research methods. We traveled internationally to expand our knowledge. We walked through the bookcase where Anne and the others entered the annex. We visited numerous Holocaust sites, memorials, and museums. We learned about the centuries of discrimination and violence inflicted upon the Jews before the Holocaust, and the more than 40,000 places where they and others were incarcerated and murdered.

We can't claim—nor is it our goal to claim—that this study changed the lives of any teachers or students (even though there are traces of life-changing moments in teachers' and students' words, artwork, and actions), but we can attest to how it changed our knowledge and positions as educators. This is not an easy inquiry for us, and we continue to grapple with basic questions shared by many (including the students) about the Holocaust: Why did so many countries stand by, and even deliberately refuse to act? How can we make sense of perpetrators, who we know had multi-dimensional identities that included committing heinous acts and loving their own families, among many conflicting positions? When will anti-Semitism finally end? What atrocities and genocides are happening currently in our world and how can we continue to live privileged lives knowing even a little about them?

True inquiries always end with more questions than answers. In addition to our questions related to the Holocaust and motivated by *The Diary of a Young Girl*, are questions about pedagogy and theory:

- How can we expand layering literacies with additional arts—music, dance, sculpture? We can only imagine the insights for students and teachers. How much art does one need to know in order to capitalize on its potential in classrooms?
- What other stories about "one" enhance students' study of the Holocaust?
- What learning happens when students stand next to strong historical and fictional characters?
- Given the powerful learning afforded by the arts, how do we pull the arts from the extra-curricular margins to the center of teaching and learning?
- What kinds of professional support will be most helpful to teachers who want to take risks with challenging texts in visual, embodied, and emotional ways? We invite you to share your experiences with us as you invite students to see, be, and feel the text.

We stand next to those from whom we have learned enduring lessons throughout this project.

We stand next to Calvin
who taught us that learning about the Holocaust is hard;
We stand next to Lucy
who found in her arts-based learning about the Holocaust an occasion to claim
her Jewish identity;
We stand next to Liam
who identified the Holocaust as a useful scar we can't forget;
We stand next to so many students
who taught us about respect and remind us that they can, and want to address
difficult topics and challenging texts; and
We stand next to the teachers, teaching artists, and guests in these classrooms
who embraced risk and had the courage to share their stories.

REFERENCES

Frank, A. (1952). *The diary of a young girl.* New York, NY: Bantam.

Schweber, S. (2006). "Holocaust fatigue": Teaching it today. *Social Education, 70*(1), 48–55.

Smith, F. D., & Grossman, M. (2008). *My secret camera: Life in the Łódź ghetto.* London, UK: Frances Lincoln Children's Books.

Appendix A
Directions for Arts-Based Instructional Strategies

ARCHIVES

Description: A visual arts activity that promotes empathy through the juxtaposition of images.
Duration: 30 minutes of online research, 15 minutes of archival photographic research.
Procedure: Identify a vetted archive of online photographs related to the challenging topic you're studying. Ask students to find photos of people or places that connect to their lives and report back about them to the rest of the class. Then, invite students to find comparable images of themselves, their families, or their local communities for each of the archive photographs. Use a bulletin board to juxtapose the sets of images and invite viewers to consider both the similarities and differences.
Reflection: How does your reading of each photograph change when positioned next to another photograph of a similar-looking person, place, or time? What do these pairs of photographs tell us about the challenging texts we're considering in our study?

Note: Thanks to Fred Whittaker for introducing this activity to us during the Anne Frank: Bearing Witness Project.

CORDEL

Description: A string stretched between two posts for hanging texts and art in the classroom.
Duration: Varies.
Procedure: The cordel is a simple construction of a clothesline and clothespins that can be used in a variety of ways to display student work and to delineate a space for performances. You could install a permanent cordel in your classroom. Stand two pieces of painted wood on opposite sides of a wall, floor to ceiling. Attach a string to one side of the wood panel at the top of the wall and then attached to the other side but a little lower, continuing to form a zigzag pattern of string down the wall so that work might be hung at every level from the floor to the ceiling. You could use fishing line, which seems invisible instead of string. Your cordel can also be permanently installed in the school's hallway, and students post work on it as a way of building a learning community *across* classrooms. Whether temporary or permanent, the wall becomes a beautiful gallery as various student work and visual and verbal texts are hung from it.

It's important that the work displayed on a cordel is of a quality and nature that an audience is compelled to experience it. The overall aesthetic of the cordel needs to be considered as the assignment is created. The cordel is most effective when meaningful work is shared among the students and with a wider audience. Your cordel could be positioned so that materials can be read from both sides.

Reflection: How were the items on the cordel connected? What did it feel like to stand and read together? How does the experience change when you can view information from both sides?

Adapted from the ArtsLiteracy Project's Handbook (www.artslit.org).

DRAMATIC AND STAGED PERFORMANCES

Description: Dramatic Performances are process-focused classroom performances that may or may not have an audience. Staged Performances may be revised and rehearsed several times before being performed formally in front of an audience.

Duration: 10 minutes to several weeks.

Procedure: Select a meaningful passage or short text for students to dramatize. Ask them to read the text and incorporate other elements from drama methods such as tableau, pantomime, and choral reading to enact an interpretation of the text with their bodies, voices, movement, and gesture. Students may play with different levels in order to convey the message they read in the text. Their dramatic performances may be literal or abstract responses to the text. Check in with students as they brainstorm and revise and invite reflections about the process and the group's intentions at the end of class.

Build on insights from dramatic performances to revise the group's work into a polished staged performance and invite audience members in addition to students to attend. Staged performances can be delivered in a classroom at the end of class, at the end of a semester, or in front of an entire community in the school's theater or cafeteria. Invite feedback from the audience members to help students see how their performances were received and how they might restructure them for future audiences. Staged performances challenge students to become texts to be read among other texts in a multimodal ensemble. After practicing, select students to direct such shows and co-construct with their classmates the sequences of performances and rationalize how that sequence supports the theme of the entire class's staged performance.

Reflection: How did you arrive at the final version of your performance? What important changes did you make to your dramatic performance and why did you make them? What did audience feedback teach you?

ICONS

Description: Construction paper silhouettes that visually symbolize linguistic representations.

Duration: 30 minutes.

Procedure: In small groups, invite students to select key words or phrases from the text and scatter them in the center of the table. If students use the same words at each table, they will end up with multiple visual interpretations of the same text. Students then browse through the words and phrases and make sure they know the meanings. They can ask each other or consult dictionaries. You may want to review any unfamiliar words with the entire class.

Students select a word or phrase and cut out a silhouette representing that word from black construction paper. Silhouettes can be glued onto tan paper or hung directly onto windows or walls around the room, or on a cordel. The class will end up with an art installation that is a visual architecture of the story that can be read and studied. For example, in pairs, students can browse the completed exhibit of silhouettes and discuss the phrases and words that are represented visually. Silhouettes can also serve as content to be dramatized in pantomimes or dramatic performances.

Reflection: How do the icons work individually? Collectively? Why/how do the icons that represented the same work look so differently?

Adapted from the ArtsLiteracy Project's Handbook (www.artslit.org).

PANTOMIME

Description: Storytelling through movement and gesture (but not words).
Duration: 30 minutes.
Procedure: Select especially important, critical, or difficult passages from the text you are studying. Place students into small groups of three to four persons and challenge them to convey the essence of the text using movement and gesture, but not words. Students may spend up to 10 minutes reading, rereading, and brainstorming ways to communicate written ideas using their bodies. Students recast meanings across the linguistic sign system of the text into the visual and gestural sign systems highlighted in pantomime. In so doing, they may generate new understandings about the text and communicate new interpretations of its meaning in ways that might not be possible when only using language. You may jigsaw a longer text or invite students to pantomime the same text in order to consider how different groups conveyed the essence of the text differently.
Reflection: What did you understand about the pantomimed text that you didn't consider in the original written text? How did your classmates use their bodies and movement to communicate?

SCULPTURE GARDEN

Description: Body-generated sculptures of words, images, or themes from a text.
Duration: 30 minutes.
Procedure: Pair students. One person in each pair chooses to be a "sculptor"; the other becomes "clay." When you call out a word or phrase, the sculptor molds the clay into its representation. Silence is maintained throughout. Music provides a mood-setting background for this activity. Once "sculpted," the clay remains frozen. On a signal from you or another facilitator, sculptors wander the garden, observing their creations.

Later the sculptor and clay exchange roles and repeat the activity. After students have worked in pairs, two groups may join together and a sculptor may work with three "pieces of clay." This provides the beginning of groups forming into tableaux. You may want to offer sculptors the opportunity to sculpt by gesture rather than touch.
Reflection: Describe similarities and differences as well as notable examples of the images that were created.

Adapted from the ArtsLiteracy Project's Handbook (www.artslit.org).

SOUND SYMPHONY

Description: An activity for building a sense of ensemble and for careful listening.
Duration: 30 minutes.
Procedure: Invite half of the students to form a circle within a larger circle and sit on the floor with legs crossed. The outside circle will monitor the process of the group in the inner circle and

share what they noticed afterwards. Ask all students to close their eyes. Working with just the inner circle, explain that when you tap a student once, he or she will begin making a repeatable sound (it can be physical or vocal). When you tap a student once again, he or she will change the sound entirely. When you tap a student twice he or she will be silent. Begin the activity when all students are silent. Tap students very slowly adding one at a time until all the students are in the symphony. Then tap students again changing sounds. Then, slowly, take everyone out. The entire symphony might last about 5 minutes.

Next, you can reverse inner and outer circles and repeat. Once a class has mastered this activity, you can ask them to work as an ensemble with no conductor. The ensemble decides through careful listening when to start, how they would like their sounds to change throughout, and when to end.

Variations:

- Have students conduct the group.
- Change the focus of the outer circle. For instance, ask them to describe a story they hear in the sounds.
- Use actual percussive or real instruments to create the improvised symphony.
- Have students perform sounds for a specific real or imagined place or event, such as the setting of a section of a piece of literature.

Reflection: What did you notice about the inner circle symphony? When did you hear the tempo change? How did different sounds affect you as a listener differently?

Reprinted from the ArtsLiteracy Project's Handbook (www.artslit.org).

TABLEAU

Description: A tableau is a frozen image of an event, activity, or concept made by one or more bodies working together.

Duration: 20 minutes.

Procedure: Organize small groups of four to six students. Invite them to form a tableau that may reflect the vision of one student or a collective creation of the group. Before beginning the activity, offer a simple set of guidelines, suggesting, for example, that everyone in the tableau is physically connected or positioned at different levels in space. Many variations are possible, including creating snapshots—tableaux presented in a series with carefully orchestrated transitions—or tableaux that move or speak.

Music played as tableaux are formed and displayed to the group contributes to the activity. When the activity is completed, lead a discussion about the content and the process to increase awareness and understanding.

Reflection: Where did we see similarities across the images? Where did we see variations? What are the limitations of tableaux? Did those limitations help you or hinder you?

Adapted from the ArtsLiteracy Project's Handbook (www.artslit.org).

Appendix B
Picturebooks and Adolescent Literature About the Holocaust

Renita Schmidt

(Titles discussed within Chapter 6 are indicated with an asterisk.)

Biography and Autobiography

*Adler, D. A. (2002). *A hero and the Holocaust: The story of Janusz Korczak and his children.* Illus. B. Farnsworth. New York, NY: Holiday House.

*Bogacki, T. (2009). *The champion of children: The story of Janusz Korczak.* New York, NY: Francis Foster Books.

*Cohen-Janca, I. (2015). *Mister doctor: Janusz Korczak and the orphans of the Warsaw ghetto.* Illus. M.A.C. Quarello (P. Ayer, trans.). Toronto, ON, Canada: Annick Press.

Ludwig, T. (2014). *Gifts from the enemy.* Illus. C. Orback. Ashland, OR: White Cloud Press.

Mata, C. (1993). *Daniel's story.* New York, NY: Scholastic.

McCann, M. R. (as told by Luba Tryszynska-Frederick) (2003). *Luba: The angel of Bergen Belsen.* Berkeley, CA: Tricycle Press.

Millman, I. (2005). *Hidden child.* New York, NY: Frances Foster Books.

*Rubin, S. G. (2006). *The cat with the yellow star: Coming of age in Terezin.* New York, NY: Holiday House.

Rubin, S. G. (2011). *Irena Sendler and the children of the Warsaw Ghetto.* Illus. B. Farnsworth. New York, NY: Holiday House.

Graphic Novel

Dauvillier, L., & Salsedo, G. (2015). *Hidden.* Illus. M. Lizano. New York, NY: First Second.

Spiegelman, A. (1991a). *Maus: A survivor's tale. My father bleeds history.* New York, NY: Pantheon Books.

Spiegelman, A. (1991b). *Maus II: A survivor's tale and here my troubles began.* New York, NY: Pantheon Books.

Historical Fiction

*Bishop, C. H. (1952). *Twenty and ten.* Illus. W. P. du Bois. New York, NY: Scholastic.

*Boyne, J. (2007). *The boy in the striped pajamas.* Oxford, UK: David Fickling Books.

Bunting, E. (1980). *Terrible things: An allegory of the Holocaust.* Illus. S. Gammell. Philadephia, PA: The Jewish Publication Society.

Bunting, E. (2002). *One candle.* Illus. W. K. Popp. New York, NY: HarperCollins.

Chotjewitz, D. (2000). *Daniel half human: And the good Nazi.* (D. Orgel, trans.). New York, NY: Atheneum Books.

*Hesse, M. (2016). *The girl in the blue coat.* Boston, MA: Little, Brown and Company.

Lasky, K. (2013). *The extra.* Somerville, MA: Candlewick Press.

Lowry, L. (1989). *Number the stars.* New York, NY: Yearling.

Morpurgo, M. (1990). *Waiting for Anya*. New York, NY: Viking.

Morpurgo, M. (2014). *Half a man*. Illus. G. O'Callaghan. Somerville, MA: Candlewick Press.

Nielsen, J. A. (2015). *A night divided*. New York, NY: Scholastic.

Rappaport, D. (2005). *The secret Seder*. Illus. E. A. McCully. New York, NY: Hyperion Books.

Reiss, J. (1972). *The upstairs room*. New York, NY: HarperCollins.

Roy, J. (2006). *Yellow star*. Tarrytown, NY: Marshall Cavendish.

Russo, M. (2005). *Always remember me: How one family survived World War II*. New York, NY: Atheneum Books for Young Readers.

Russo, M. (2011). *I will come back for you: A family in hiding during World War II*. New York, NY: Schwartz & Wade Books.

Spinelli, J. (2005). *Milkweed*. New York, NY: Scholastic.

Vos, I. (1996). *The key is lost*. Illus. T. Edelstein. New York, NY: HarperCollins.

Yolen, J. (2004). *The devil's arithmetic*. New York, NY: Puffin.

Zusak, M. (2007). *The book thief*. New York, NY: Knopf Books for Young Readers.

Memoir

Arato, R. (2013). *The last train: A Holocaust story*. Toronto, ON, Canada: Owl Kids.

Bitton-Jackson, L. (1997). *I have lived a thousand years: Growing up in the Holocaust*. New York, NY: Simon & Schuster Books for Young Readers.

Gruenbaum, M. (2015). *Somewhere there is still a sun: A memoir of the Holocaust*. New York, NY: Aladdin.

Leyson, L. (2013). *The boy on the wooden box: How the impossible became possible…on Schindler's list*. New York, NY: Atheneum Books for Young Readers.

Wiesel, E. (1972). *Night*. New York, NY: Hill and Wang.

Myth

*Deedy, C. A. (2000). *The yellow star: The legend of King Christian X of Denmark*. Illus. H. Sørensen. Atlanta, GA: Peachtree.

Non-Fiction

Adler, D. A. (1987). *The number on my grandfather's arm*. Photos by Rose Eichenbaum. New York, NY: UAHC Press.

*Adler, D. A. (1997). *Hiding from the Nazis*. Illus. K. Ritz. New York, NY: Holiday House.

Bachrach, S. D. (1994). *Tell them we remember: The story of the Holocaust*. Boston, MA: Little, Brown and Company.

*Bartoletti, S. C. (2005). *Hitler youth: Growing up in Hitler's shadow*. New York, NY: Scholastic.

*Bartoletti, S. C. (2008). *The boy who dared*. New York, NY: Scholastic.

Borden, L. (2005). *The journey that saved Curious George: The true wartime escape of Margret and H.A. Rey*. Illus. A. Drummond. Boston, MA: Houghton Mifflin Company.

*Freedman, R. (2016). *We will not be silent: The White Rose student resistance movement that defied Adolf Hitler*. New York, NY: Clarion.

Hodge, D. (2012). *Rescuing the children: The story of the kindertransport*. Toronto, ON, Canada: Tundra Books.

Hoose, P. (2015). *The boys who challenged Hitler: Knud Pedersen and the Churchill Club*. New York, NY: Farrar, Straus and Giroux.

Krinitz, E. N., & Steinhardt, B. (2005). *Memories of survival*. New York, NY: Hyperion Books for Children.

Levine, K. (2002). *Hana's suitcase: A true story*. New York, NY: Scholastic.

*Rubin, S. G. (2000). *Fireflies in the dark: The story of Friedl Dicker-Brandeis and the children of Terezin*. New York, NY: Holiday House.

Rubin, S. G. (2005). *The flag with fifty-six stars: A gift from the survivors of Mauthausen*. Illus. B. Farnsworth. New York, NY: Holiday House.

*Thomson, R. (2011). *Terezín: Voices from the Holocaust.* Somerville, MA: Candlewick Press.

Picturebook

Elvgren, J. (2014). *The whispering town.* Illus. F. Santomauro. Minneapolis, MN: Kar-Ben Publishing.

*Gallaz, C., & Innocenti, R. (1985). *Rose Blanche.* Illus. R. Innocenti. Mankato, MN: Creative Editions.

*Gottesfeld, J. (2016). *The tree in the courtyard: Looking through Anne Frank's window.* Illus. P. McCarty. New York, NY: Knopf Books for Young Readers.

Hausfater, R. (2001). *The little boy star: An allegory of the Holocaust.* Illus. O. Latyk. Berkeley, CA: Milk and Cookies Press.

Hesse, K. (2004). *The cats in Krasinski square.* Illus. W. Watson. New York, NY: Scholastic Press.

*Johnston, T. (2004). *The harmonica.* Illus. R. Mazallen. Watertown, MA: Charlesbridge.

Kacer, K. (2014). *The magician of Auschwitz.* Illus. G. Newland. Toronto, ON, Canada: Second Story Press.

Lakin, P. (1994). *Don't forget.* Illus. T. Rand. New York, NY: Tambourine Books.

Lewis, J. P. (2015). *The wren and the sparrow.* Illus. Y. Nayberg. Minneapolis, MN: Kar-Ben Publishing.

Nerlove, M. (1996). *Flowers on the wall.* New York, NY: McElderry Books.

*Oppenheim, S. L. (1992). *The lily cupboard.* Illus. R. Himler. New York, NY: HarperCollins.

Polacco, P. (2000). *The butterfly.* New York, NY: Philomel Books.

Schnur, S. (1995). *The tie man's miracle: A Chanukah tale.* Illus. S. T. Johnson. New York, NY: Morrow Junior Books.

Ungerer, T. (1999). *Otto: The autobiography of a teddy bear.* New York, NY: Phaidon Press.

Vander Zee, R. V. (2003). *Erika's story.* Illus. R. Innocenti. Mankato, MN: Creative Editions.

*Wiviott, M. (2010). *Benno and the night of broken glass.* Illus. J. Bisaillon. Minneapolis, MN: Kar-Ben Publishing.

Poetry

*Volavková, H. (Ed.). (1962). *I never saw another butterfly: Children's drawings and poems from Terezin concentration camp 1942–1944.* New York, NY: McGraw-Hill.

Wiviott, M. (2015). *Paper hearts.* New York, NY: Margaret K. McElderry Books.

More Literature Featuring Anne Frank

Anne Frank House (1994). *Anne Frank: 1929–1945.* Amsterdam, The Netherlands: The Anne Frank House.

Jacobson, S., & Colón, E. (2010). *Anne Frank: The Anne Frank House authorized graphic biography.* New York, NY: Farrar, Straus & Giroux.

McDonough, Y. Z. (1997). *Anne Frank.* New York, NY: Henry Holt and Company.

Rubin, S. G. (2009). *The Anne Frank case: Simon Wiesenthal's search for the truth.* New York, NY: Holiday House.

Van der Rol, R., & Verhoeven, R. (1992). *Anne Frank: Beyond the diary.* New York, NY: Scholastic Inc.

Appendix C
Additional Challenging Texts
Some Recommendations
Renita Schmidt, James S. Chisholm, and Kathryn F. Whitmore

(Titles discussed within Chapter 6 are indicated with an asterisk.)

Biography

*Cline-Ransome, L. (2015). *My story, my dance: Robert Battle's journey to Alvin Ailey*. New York, NY: Simon & Schuster.

*Engle, M. (2015). *Drum dream girl: How one girl's courage changed music*. Illus. R. López. New York, NY: Houghton Mifflin Harcourt.

Fiction

Adichie, C. N. (2003). *Purple hibiscus*. Chapel Hill, NC: Algonquin.

Anderson, L. H. (1999). *Speak*. New York, NY: Penguin.

*Budhos, M. (2016). *Watched*. New York, NY: Wendy Lamb Books.

Dawe, T. (2012). *Into the river*. Wellington, NZ: Mangakino University Press.

Erskine, K. (2010). *Mockingbird*. New York, NY: Philomel.

Fraillon, Z. (2016). *The bone sparrow*. London, UK: Orion Children's Books.

Gratz, A. (2017). *Refugee*. New York, NY: Scholastic.

*Magoon, K. (2014). *How it went down*. New York, NY: Henry Holt.

McCormick, P. (2006). *Sold*. New York, NY: Hyperion.

Na, A. (2001). *A step from heaven*. New York, NY: Penguin Putnam.

Olson, G. (2007). *Call me hope*. New York, NY: Little, Brown and Company.

Placide, J. (2002). *Fresh girl*. New York, NY: Wendy Lamb Books.

Polonsky, A. (2014). *Gracefully Grayson*. New York, NY: Hyperion.

Reynolds, J., & Kiely, B. (2015). *All American boys*. New York, NY: Simon & Shuster Children's Publishing Division.

Rowell, R. (2013). *Eleanor & Park*. New York, NY: St. Martin's Press.

Saenz, B. A. (2012). *Aristotle and Dante discover the secrets of the universe*. New York, NY: Simon & Shuster Children's Publishing Division.

Trueman, T. (2000). *Stuck in neutral*. New York, NY: HarperCollins.

Graphic Novel

*Brown, D. (2016). *Drowned city: Hurricane Katrina & New Orleans*. New York, NY: Houghton Mifflin Harcourt.

Neri, G. (2010). *Yummy: The last days of a southside shorty*. Illus. R. DuBurke. New York, NY: Lee & Low.

Satrapi, M. (2007). *The complete Persepolis*. New York, NY: Pantheon.

Historical Fiction

*Engle, M. (2014). *Silver people: Voices from the Panama Canal*. New York, NY: Houghton Mifflin Harcourt.
Rhodes, J. P. (2010). *Ninth ward*. New York, NY: Little, Brown and Company.
Rhodes, J. P. (2016). *Towers falling*. New York, NY: Little, Brown and Company.
*Sepetys, R. (2016). *Salt to the sea*. New York, NY: Philomel Books.

Memoir

*Barakat, I. (2016). *Balcony on the moon*. New York, NY: Farrar, Straus and Giroux.
*Lee, S., & McClelland, S. E. (2016). *Every falling star*. New York, NY: Harry N. Abrams.

Non-Fiction

Ellis, D. (2013). *Looks like daylight: Voices of indigenous kids*. Toronto, ON: Groundwood Books.
*Lewis, J. P., & Lyon, G. E. (2014). *Voices from the march on Washington*. New York, NY: Boyds Mills/
    WordSong.
*Weatherford, C. B. (2016). *Freedom in Congo Square*. Illus. G. Christie. New York, NY: Little Bee Books.

Picturebook

*Buitrago, J. (2015). *Two white rabbits*. Illus. R. Yockteng. Toronto, ON: Groundwood Press.
*Ruurs, M. (2016). *Stepping stones: A refugee family's journey*. (F. Raheem, Trans.). Illus. A. Bardr. Victoria,
    BC: Orca Press.

Play

Kaufman, M., and the Members of Tectonic Theater Project. (2001). *The Laramie project*. New York, NY:
    Vintage.

Novel in Verse

Alexander, K. (2014). *The crossover*. New York, NY: Houghton Mifflin Harcourt.
Clark, K. E. (2013). *Freakboy*. New York, NY: Farrar, Straus and Giroux.
Napoli, D. J. (1997). *Stones in water*. New York, NY: Dutton Children's Books.

Index